PREFACE.

STATE OF NEW YORK,
IN SENATE, ALBANY, *April* 26, 1870.

On motion of Mr. GENET,

Resolved, That there be prepared and printed, under the direction of the clerk of the Senate, a continuation of the Digest of Claims, compiled in the year 1865, which shall comprise all claims presented in either branch of the Legislature, with a brief statement of the nature of the claim, whether for land or water damages, or for extra compensation upon canal contracts, and what legislative action, if any, was had thereon; including and specifying therein all claims which have been allowed, or otherwise disposed of, with the amount named in bills which have been passed as an absolute appropriation, or as the maximum limit of an award, and the amount awarded in any case by the Canal Appraisers or the Canal Board. Such Digest shall also include all awards, either by the Canal Appraisers or the Canal Board, made since the publication of said Digest of 1865, on claim bills passed previous thereto but not included therein.

Resolved, That the Canal Appraisers and the Canal Board be requested to furnish such information as may be in their possession, to render the proposed Digest as complete as possible.

Resolved, That five hundred copies of the Digest, prepared as above directed, be printed and bound for the use of the Legislature, under the direction of the clerk, as soon as possible after the completion thereof, and previous to the meeting of the next Legislature.

By order.

HIRAM CALKINS,
Clerk.

PREFACE.

In obedience to the foregoing resolution, this Digest has been prepared. The form and manner of the compilation of previous Digests, made by order of the Senate, has been maintained, and no effort spared in this "continuation" to render it as perfect a record of the claims as the means at command would allow.

The present work contains all the petitions and claims of every character presented to the Senate from 1866 to 1870, inclusive, together with the legislative action thereon, and the awards made since the issue of the last Digest. A resolution passed the Assembly, at its last session, directing the clerk of that body to prepare a Digest of all claims presented to the Assembly, with the legislative action thereon, for the same period. It is, therefore, thought best not to duplicate the matter by including the claims introduced in the Assembly in this Digest. This work, therefore, is confined to the claims presented to the Senate.

It also contains a supplement, in which there will be found a compilation of all claims presented to, determined by, and pending before, either the Canal Board or Canal Appraisers, with their decisions and amounts awarded in each case for the last five years.

This compilation has been prepared, under my direction and supervision, by OLIVER C. BENTLEY and CHARLES J. GAYLORD, from the records of the Legislature and Canal Department.

HIRAM CALKINS.

ALBANY, *January* 1*st*, 1871.

DIGEST OF CLAIMS

AND THE ACTION THEREON BY THE

Legislature and the Canal Board

TOGETHER WITH THE AWARDS MADE BY THE
BOARD OF CANAL APPRAISERS;
ALSO A SUPPLEMENT
SHOWING THE CLAIMS PRESENTED, DETERMINED
AND PENDING BEFORE THE CANAL BOARD
AND THE CANAL APPRAISERS,
FROM
1866 TO 1870, INCLUSIVE

COMPILED UNDER THE AUTHORITY OF A RESOLUTION OF THE SENATE OF THE
STATE OF NEW YORK, PASSED APRIL 26, 1870, UNDER THE DIRECTION OF

Hiram Calkins

CLERK OF SENATE

HERITAGE BOOKS
2012

HERITAGE BOOKS
AN IMPRINT OF HERITAGE BOOKS, INC.

Books, CDs, and more—Worldwide

For our listing of thousands of titles see our website
at
www.HeritageBooks.com

A Facsimile Reprint
Published 2012 by
HERITAGE BOOKS, INC.
Publishing Division
100 Railroad Ave. #104
Westminster, Maryland 21157

Originally published
Albany:
The Argus Company, Printers
1870

— Publisher's Notice —
In reprints such as this, it is often not possible to remove blemishes from the original. We feel the contents of this book warrant its reissue despite these blemishes and hope you will agree and read it with pleasure.

International Standard Book Numbers
Paperbound: 978-0-7884-1235-6
Clothbound: 978-0-7884-9455-0

DIGEST OF CLAIMS.

Thomas Aash.

(See John C. Blaisdell and others.)

Charles H. Adams.

Nature of Claim:

Damages for loss of bridge over Champlain canal.

Legislative Action:

Senate Journal, 1867. Petition presented and referred to the committee on claims, 169. Committee on claims discharged from further consideration of the petition, and the same referred to the committee on canals, 240. Committee reported favorably by bill. Read twice and referred to the committee of the whole, 719.

Walter S. Alden.

(See Erskine G. Clark and others.)

Thomas C. Alliger.

(See Linus R. Clark and others.)

Trustees of Amsterdam and Port Jackson.

Nature of Claim:

Compensation for damages sustained in loss of bridge over the Mohawk river, in the spring of 1865.

Legislative Action:

Senate Journal, 1866. Petition presented and referred to the committee on claims. Reported favorably by bill and referred to the committee of the whole, 125. Ordered to a third reading, 148. Bill passed, 157. (See Senate document No. 23, 1866.)

Assembly Journal, 1866. Bill received and referred to the committee on claims, 321. Reported favorably and referred to the committee of the whole, 540. Ordered to a third reading, 729. Bill passed, 846.

Under this act no award has yet been made.

John Anderson.

(See Linus R. Clark and others.)

George B. Anderson.

(See Linus R. Clark and others.)

Rensselaer W. Angel.

Nature of Claim:

Damages to premises of petitioner, in the town of Belfast, Allegany county, by reason of a break in the Genesee Valley canal.

Legislative Action:

Senate Journal, 1866. Petition presented and referred to the committee on claims.

John H. Anthon.

Nature of Claim:

For the return of money paid by him for auction fees.

Legislative Action:

Senate Journal, 1868. Petition presented and referred to the committee on finance, 141.

L. G. Avery and others.

Nature of Claim:

Compensation for damages to their salt blocks, caused by raising the banks and waters of the Oswego canal.

Legislative Action:

Senate Journal, 1866. Petition presented and referred to the committee on claims, 438.

H. H. Babcock and Son.
(See Linus R. Clark and others.)

Black River Claims.

(Senate Digest, year 1869.)

Bagley and Sewall.

(See Linus R. Clark and others.)

Franklin Bailey.

(See John C. Blaisdell and others.)

Harden Bailey.

(See John C. Blaisdell and others.)

Alonzo Banks.

(See Ovid Plumb and others.)

Myron Bangs.

(See Joseph A. Scoville.)

Nicholas Barhydt.

Nature of Claim:

Compensation for land taken in the enlargement of the Erie canal, at Schenectady.

Legislative Action:

Senate Journal, 1866. Petition presented and referred to the committee on claims. Reported by bill and referred to the committee of the whole, 632. Ordered to a third reading, 780. Bill passed, 796.

Assembly Journal, 1866. Bill received and referred to the committee on claims, 1444. Committee reported favorably. Bill referred to the committee of the whole, 1523. Bill passed, 1725.

Award:

Under this act no award has yet been made by the canal appraisers.

John Barnes.

Nature of Claim:

Damages to premises of petitioner, by reason of a break in the Erie canal, at Rochester, March, 1865.

(See B. H. Clark and others.)

Legislative Action:

Senate Journal, 1866. Petition presented and referred to the committee on claims, 94. Committee reported adversely. Report laid on the table, 442.

Alexander Barkley.

Nature of Claim:

Papers not on file, and nature of claim not known.

Legislative Action:

Senate Journal, 1870. Bill introduced and referred to the committee on claims, 742.

Peter Barker.

(See John C. Blaisdell and others.)

Z. W. Barrett.

Nature of Claim:

Compensation for damages to his lands, caused by the overflow of the waters of the Genesee Valley canal.

Legislative Action:

Senate Journal, 1868. Petition presented and referred to the committee on claims, 98. Notice of bill for payment of damages to Zaccheus W. Barrett, William Huggins and John Roberts, 101. Bill introduced and referred to the committee on claims, 105.

Eloisa O. Beebe.

(See Willis B. Sayre and others.)

Charles Belling.

(See Giles Shell and others.)

James Bellows.

Nature of Claim :

Additional compensation for labor performed under contract for keeping the Chemung canal and feeder in repair, on account of improvement in Chemung river, at Corning, in the summer and fall of 1864.

Legislative Action :

Senate Journal, 1866. Petition presented and referred to the committee on claims, 266. Committee reported by bill, entitled "an act for the relief of Jarvis Lord, assignee of James Bellows," and referred to committee of the whole, 583.

(See Jarvis Lord.)

Albert Bennett and others.

Nature of Claim :

For the payment to the petitioners of bounties received by the town of Nelson from the State.

Legislative Action :

Senate Journal, 1866. Petition presented and referred to the committee on the judiciary, 36. Committee reported adversely. Report agreed to, 497.

Senate Journal, 1867. Papers on file referred to the committee on judiciary, 128. Reported adversely. Laid on the table, 304.

Charles Berry.
(See Linus R. Clark and others.)

Zarah Berry.

(See E. D. Sherwood and others.)

Olive Biddlecome.

(See J. J. Burton and others.)

Lucien Billinghurst, Erastus Knapp, Jefferson Johnson, Orrin W. Rose and John G. Wormley.

Nature of Claim:

Compensation for the loss of a quantity of hemlock timber, carried away by the freshet of March 17, 1865, at Corning; owing, as alleged, to the defective docking and embankment of the Chemung river, in connection with the Chemung canal.

Legislative Action:

Senate Journal, 1869. Petition presented and referred to the committee on claims, 73. Bill introduced and referred to the committee on claims, 85. Committee reported by bill, which was committed to the committee of the whole, 138. Ordered to a third reading, 303. Passed, 308.

Assembly Journal, 1869. Bill received and referred to the committee on claims, 590. Referred to the committee of the whole, 691. Ordered to a third reading, 697. Lost, 827. Reconsidered and passed, 1351.

Under this act the canal appraisers have made the following awards:

	Amount claimed.	Amount allowed.
Lucien Billinghurst	$276 00	$367 77
Erastus Knapp	400 00	373 10
Jefferson Johnson	810 00	1079 32
Orrin W. Rose	1750 00	2331 87
John G. Wormley	260 00	266 50

(See Laws of 1869, chapter 588.)

Walter Bissell.

(Representatives, personal, of Walter Bissell, deceased.)

(See John Harvey.)

Black River Claims.

(See Linus W. Clark and others.)

John C. Blaisdell, Harden Bailey and others.

Thomas Aash, Shimuel Griffen, Ashael P. Dewey, Porter Barker, Joseph C. Moore, Oliver Butterfield, Samuel H. Harden, Henry Bruon, George Halley, Franklin Bailey, Ephraim P. Huestis, John Graham, George Ingalls, Campbell and Thompson, Michael Minton, Robert Nichols, Jr., Charles T. Wright, John Miller, Terence Daly, Alexander Kincade and George F. Dudley.

Nature of Claims:

Compensation for damages to their lands, overflowed by

the waters of the Champlain canal, in the towns of Kingsbury and Fort Ann, Washington county.

Legislative Action:

Senate Journal, 1869. Bill introduced and referred to the committee on claims, 778. Assembly bill received and referred to the committee on claims, 1019. Reported complete and ordered to a third reading, 1082. Bill passed, 1095.

Assembly Journal, 1869. Petition presented and referred to the committee on claims. Reported favorably and committed to committee of the whole, 786. (See Assembly document No. 131.) Ordered to a third reading, 1797. Bill passed, 1866. (See Laws of 1869, chapter 785.)

Under this act the following awards have been made:

	Amount claimed.	Amount allowed.
John C. Blaisdell	$230 00	$278 30
Oliver Butterfield	330 00	399 30
George Ingalls	320 00	387 00
Terence Daly	390 00	471 90
Alexander Kincade	980 00	1185 80

J. Blood.

(See Linus R. Clark and others.)

Augustus Botsford.

(See Ovid Plumb and others.)

M. N. Bradley.

Nature of Claim:

Papers not found on file, and nature of claim not known.

Legislative Action:

Senate Journal, 1866. Notice of bill, 34.

George B. Bradley.

Nature of Claim:

(See John McBurney.)

Legislative Action:

Senate Journal, 1866. Petition presented and referred to the committee on claims, 254.

Daniel Bread and others.

Nature of Claim:

Papers not found on file, and nature of claims not known.

Legislative Action:

Senate Journal, 1866. Petition presented, and referred to the committee on Indian affairs, 52, 64. Committee report, that chapter 58, of Laws of 1839, confer, etc., and ask to be discharged, etc. Report agreed to, and committee discharged, 88.

George G. Breed and Oliver Breed.
(See Theodocia Wall and others.)

H. S. Briggs.

(See Linus R. Clark and others.)

Eli A. Bronson.

Nature of Claim:

Compensation for damages occasioned by the removal of a dock, by the State authorities, at Geneva.

Legislative Action:

Senate Journal, 1867. Petition presented and referred to the committee on claims, 239. Committee reported adversely, in writing, and report agreed to, 968. (See Senate document No. 40.)

Senate Journal, 1868. Papers taken from files and referred to the committee on claims, 323. Reported favorably by bill, and committed to the committee of the whole, 337. Ordered to a third reading, 844. Passed, 852. (See Senate Document No. 65.)

Assembly Journal, 1868. Bill received and referred to the committee on claims, 1412. Reported favorably, and committed to the committee of the whole, 1572. Ordered to a third reading and lost.

Senate Journal, 1869. Papers taken from files and referred to the committee on claims. Committee reported by bill and committed to the committee of the whole, 80. Ordered to a third reading, 98. Bill passed, 104.

Assembly Journal, 1869. Bill received and referred to the committee on claims, 179. Reported favorably and committed to the committee of the whole, 691. Ordered to a third reading, 1156. Bill passed, 1455. (See Laws of 1869, chapter 587.)

Amount claimed, $756.90. Under this act the Canal Appraisers allowed the sum of $978.78.

Enos C. Brooks and William S. Fullerton.

Nature of Claim:

For the reimbursement of moneys expended by them and services in raising the 64th and 130th regiments, N. Y. S. V., in 1861 and 1862.

Legislative Action:

Senate Journal, 1870. Bill introduced and referred to the committee on militia, 577. Reported favorably, 764. Ordered to a third reading, 744. Bill passed, 825.

Assembly Journal, 1870. Bill received and referred to the committee on claims, 1414. Reported favorably and committed to the committee of the whole, 1638. Ordered to a third reading, 1678. Bill passed, 1853. (See Laws of 1870, chapter 481.)

By the terms of this law, the Inspector-General, Quartermaster-General, and Judge-Advocate-General, are authorized to hear this claim, and the Treasurer to pay it.

Under this act no award has yet been made.

Henry Bruon.

(See John C. Blaisdell and others.)

Timothy Buckley.

(See Erskine G. Clark and others.)

Roswell S. Burrows.

Nature of Claim:

Compensation for damages to his premises, in the village of Albion, caused by the erection of a bridge and approaches thereto, over the Erie canal, in said village.

Legislative Action:

Senate Journal, 1870. Bill introduced and referred to the committee on claims, 146. Assembly bill received and referred to the committee on canals, 656. Reported favorably and committed to the committee of the whole, 736. Ordered to a third reading, 809. Bill passed, 907.

Assembly Journal, 1870. Bill introduced and referred to the committee on claims, 427. Reported favorably and referred to the committee of the whole, 735. Ordered to a third reading, 829. Bill passed, 1038.

This bill did not become a law.

Phebe Burton, Olna Burton, David Burton.

(See J. J. Burton and others.)

Joseph J. Burton, T. Franklin Harris, J. B. Warren, W. R. Lyon, Phebe Burton, W. W. Lyon, Olna Burton, Olive Biddlecome, L. Jane B. Fowler, Robert R. Jones, Lucy E. Whitney, Stephen Card, David Burton, Susan M. Smith, Mary A. Smith, Maria Smith and Joseph Smith.

Nature of Claim:

Papers not found on file, and nature of claims not known.

Legislative Action:

Senate Journal, 1867. Bill introduced and referred to the committee on claims, 441.

Oliver Butterfield.

(See John C. Blaisdell and others.)

Richard Calrow, Jr.

Nature of Claim:

Compensation for work done on the State arsenal at New York.

Legislative Action:

Senate Journal, 1870. Petition presented and referred to the committee on claims, 51. Bill introduced, read twice and referred to the committee on claims, 79. Reported favorably and committed to the committee of the whole, 646. Ordered to a third reading, 809. Bill passed, 869.

Assembly Journal, 1870. Senate bill received and referred to the committee on judiciary, 1478. Reported favorably and recommitted to the committee, with power to report complete, 1519. Ordered to a third reading, 1567. Bill passed, 1728.

This bill did not become a law.

Campbell and Thompson.

(See John C. Blaisdell and others.)

James Campbell and John Campbell.

(See Brackett H. Clark and others.)

Stephen Card.

(See J. J. Burton and others.)

Orville N. Carlton.

(See Erskine G. Clark and others.)

George Carman.

(See Linus R. Clark and others.)

Charles Carman and Ellen A. Gutches.

Nature of Claim:

Compensation for damages sustained by reason of the leakage of the enlarged Erie canal and flowage of their lands, in the town of Mentz, Cayuga county.

Legislative Action:

Senate Journal, 1866. Petition presented and referred to the committee on claims, 31.

Charles E. Case.

Nature of Claim:

For money and interest left by him on deposit with the State, and for the amount retained monthly as security for the fulfillment of his contract as repair contractor for section No. 2, Oswego canal, together with compensation for his services for fractional part of a month.

Legislative Action:

Senate Journal, 1866. Petition presented and referred to the committee on claims, 59. Adverse report. Agreed to, 460. Motion to reconsider laid upon the table, 469. (See Senate document, No. 67, 1866.)

Senate Journal, 1867. Papers taken from the files and referred to the committee on claims, 255. Committee reported favorably in writing and by bill, and referred to the committee of the whole, 703. Ordered to a third reading, 769. Bill passed, 782. (See Senate document, No. 72.)

Assembly Journal, 1867. Petition presented and referred to the committee on claims, 666. Committee reported favorably in writing and by bill, 1042. Senate bill received and substituted, 1321. Referred to the committee on claims with power to report complete, 1549. Reported complete and ordered to a third reading, 1552. Bill passed, 1748. (See Assembly document No. 194. See Laws of 1867, chapter 900.)

Under this act the Canal Board allowed the claimant for deposits with the auditor, $4,667.24, with interest. For amount retained by the auditor from monthly compensation $2,082.56, with interest. For amount earned during the month of March, 1868, $1,026.90.

Samuel F. Case.

(See John F. Hosch.)

Lorenzo Case.

(See Linus R. Clark and others.)

Nicholas M. Catlin.

(See Erskine G. Clark and others.)

John Chadwick.

Nature of Claim:

Papers not found on file, and nature of the claim not known.

Legislative Action:

Senate Journal, 1867. Notice of bill, 156.

John Chadwick.

(See Giles Shell and others.)

Calvin T. Chamberlain.

Nature of Claim:

Compensation for damages caused by the diversion of water from his mill, on the Genesee Valley canal.

Legislative Action:

Senate Journal, 1869. Papers taken from files and referred to the committee on claims, 200.

Linus R. Clark and others.

(Black River Claims.)

Nature of Claims:

Compensation for damages occasioned by the giving way of the North Lake reservoir.

Legislative Action:

Senate Journal, 1869. Petition presented and referred to the committee on claims, 818. Committee reported by bill, which was committed to the committee of the whole, 865. All of these claims were referred to the Canal Appraisers. (See Laws of 1869, chapter 598.)

Under this act, the Board of Appraisers of 1869 made a number of awards, all of which were set aside by the Canal Board, and the claims recommitted to the Board of Appraisers of 1870. The amount claimed in each case will be found in the supplement to this digest.

Clark and Little.

(See Linus R. Clark and others.)

Erskine G. Clark and others.

Edward Gay, Joseph H. Harris, James Stack, Nelson Miller, Ezekiel Smith, Joseph Potvin, Timothy Crowley, George Herford, William Henry, George A. Underhill, Walter S. Alden, Daniel Guarin, Samuel Wood, Robert J. Peck, Sidney B. Miller, Robert Wiggins Reuben C. Oatman, John Davidson, Jeremiah F. Miller, Horace Dibble, Timothy Buckley, James Johnston, Peter Lawson, James Toole, Hugh Story, John G. Henry, Mary Henry, Orville N. Carlton, John P. Matteson, James Guarin, Andrew Parker, Bryan Daly, Alexander McKee, Thomas Gallagher, Bloomer Underhill, Nicholas M. Catlin, Patrick McIntyre and Benjamin Ferris.

Nature of Claim:

Compensation for damages sustained by them from the overflowing of the water of the Champlain canal in the town of Kingsbury, in the county of Washington.

Legislative Action :

Senate Journal, 1869. Bill introduced and referred to the committee on claims, 777.

B. H. Clark.

Nature of Claim :

Compensation for damages sustained in loss of canal boat, by reason of a break in the Erie canal, near Whitesborough, May 11, 1864.

Legislative Action :

Senate Journal, 1866. Petition presented and referred to the committee on claims, 63. Papers taken from the files and referred to the committee on claims, 67. Committee reported adversely. Report laid on the table, 442. (See Senate document No. 60.)

B. H. Clark and others.

Brackett H. Clark, Samuel D. Porter, William T. Thompson, James Campbell, John Campbell, Mortimer C. Mordoff, Elizabeth Flint, Charlotte M. Crandall, John Sheridan, John Barnes, Cornelius R. Parsons, Ambrose Crane and Mary H. Wilcox.

Nature of Claim :

Compensation for damages arising from a break in the Erie canal, at Rochester, March 18th, 1865.

Legislative Action:

Senate Journal, 1866. Petition presented and referred to the committee on claims. Committee reported adversely. Report laid on the table, 442. (See Senate document No. 62.)

Senate Journal, 1869. Papers taken from files and referred to the committee on claims, 443.

Senate Journal, 1870. Papers taken from files and referred to the committee on claims, 73.

Samuel Coe.

(See Ovid Plumb and others.)

William Cole.

(See E. D. Sherwood and others.)

James M. Coleman.

(See E. D. Sherwood and others.)

Charles A. Collamer.

Nature of Claim:

Compensation for damages to the person of claimant, and to his horses, wagon, and harness, caused by the giving way of a bridge over the Champlain canal, in July, 1866, while he was crossing said bridge, in the town of Easton.

Legislative Action:

Senate Journal, 1869. Bill introduced and referred to the committee on claims, 161. Message was sent to the Assembly for papers, 165. Committee reported adversely. Report agreed to.and the bill rejected, 264. (See Senate document No. 55, of 1869.)

John W. Conley.

Nature of Claim:

Compensation for damages to the premises of petitioner, in building a bridge and approaches over the Erie canal at Canastota.

Legislative Action:

Senate Journal, 1867. Petition presented and referred to committee on claims, 46. A message was sent to the Assembly, requesting that the papers in the matter be sent to the Senate, 48.

Charles C. Caston.

(See Ovid Plumb and others.)

Daniel Cotter.

Nature of Claim:

Compensation for damages to his boat and cargo, caused by the giving away of the lock gates of the Erie canal, at Lockport.

Legislative Action:

Senate Journal, 1870. Petition presented and referred to the committee on claims, 110. Reported favorably and committed to the committee of the whole, 435. Ordered to a third reading, 766. Bill passed, 866.

Assembly Journal, 1870. Senate bill received and referred to the committee on claims, 1479. Reported complete and ordered to a third reading, 1758. Bill passed, 1853.

This bill did not become a law.

Elizabeth Craft.

Nature of Claim:

Compensation for services of Edwin Craft, as night-guard at Sing Sing prison, for three years from the date of his death.

A bill passed both Houses.

(See Laws of 1869, chapters 251, and 554.)

By the provisions of this law, the sum of two thousand three hundred and forty dollars ($2,340) is appropriated to

Elizabeth Craft, and the Treasurer is directed to pay the same, on the warrant of the Comptroller, out of any moneys unappropriated.

Under this act, the sum of $2,340 was paid to the petitioner by the Treasurer.

Enos T. Crandall.

(See Linus R. Clark and others.)

Charlotte M. Crandall.

(See B. H. Clark and others.)

Ambrose Crane.

(See B. H. Clark and others.)

Timothy Crowley.

(See Erskine G. Clark and others.)

Nathan Crum.

Nature of Claim:

Compensation for injuries sustained in consequence of the giving way of a bridge over the Black River canal.

Legislative Action:

Senate Journal, 1870. Bill introduced and referred to the committee on claims, 373. Reported favorably and committed to the committee of the whole, 508. Ordered to a third reading, 766. Bill passed, 867.

Assembly Journal, 1870. Senate bill received and referred to the committee on claims, 1478. Reported favorably and committed to the committee of the whole, 1552. Ordered to a third reading, 1634.

C. W. Curtis.

(See Ovid Plumb and others.)

Horatio N. Curtis.

Nature of Claim:

Papers not found on file, and nature of claim not known.

Legislative Action:

Senate Journal, 1866. Papers taken from the files and referred to the committee on claims, 351.

Curtis and Flynn.

(See Linus R. Clark and others.)

Geo. M. Cuyler.

Nature of Claim:

Compensation for damages caused by the overflow of the waters of Beard's creek and Genesee Valley canal, in the years 1867, 1868 and 1869.

Legislative Action:

Senate Journal, 1870. Bill introduced and referred to the committee on canals, 216. Committee discharged and referred to the committee on claims. Reported favorably and committed to the committee of the whole, 508. Ordered to a third reading, 766. Bill passed, 868.

Assembly Journal, 1870. Senate bill received and referred to the committee on claims, 1478. Recommitted to the committee on claims, with power to report complete, 1634. Reported complete and committed to the committee of the whole, 1638.

Mary E. Daggett.

Nature of Claim:

Compensation for damages, resulting from the erection of a bridge over the Erie canal.

Legislative Action:

Senate Journal, 1867. Petition presented and referred to the committee on canals, 48.

Terrence Daley.

(See John C. Blaisdell and others.)

Bryan Daley.

(See Erskine G. Clark and others.)

Walter L. Daly.

(See Ovid Plumb and others.)

Thomas Dallamir.

(See Linus R. Clark and others.)

C. A. Danolds and M. Mills.

Nature of Claims:

For additional compensation under contract for building stone dam across Mohawk river, at Rexford flats.

Legislative Action:

Senate Journal, 1866. Petition presented and referred to the committee on claims, 119.

Danube (Town of).

(See Fink's Basin Bridge.)

John Davidson.

(See Erskine G. Clark and others.)

Davis' Sewing Machine Company.

(See Linus R. Clark and others.)

Charles Davis.

Nature of Claim:

For repayment of money paid to John H. Smith, as assistant collector, on the Chenango canal, at Binghamton; the amount to be paid (if any) not to exceed $350.

Legislative Action:

Senate Journal, 1870. Bill introduced and referred to the committee on claims, 36. Reported favorably and committed to the committee of the whole, 88. Ordered to a third reading, 152. Bill passed, 161.

Assembly Journal, 1870. Senate bill received and referred to the committee on claims. Reported favorably and committed to the committee of the whole, 736. Ordered to a third reading, 830. Bill passed. (See laws of 1870, chapter 156.)

Under this act the Canal Board allowed the sum of $333.12.

William Dean.

(See Ovid Plumb and others.)

Gerardus De Forest.

Nature of Claim:

Compensation for clothing, and damage to his business, by reason of his being drafted into the New York State militia in 1812.

Legislative Action:

Senate Journal, 1870. Petition presented and referred to the committee on claims, 153.

C. J. De Graw.

Nature of Claim:

Compensation for damages sustained by petitioner, in the loss of logs and timber in May, 1864, in consequence of not being allowed to enter the Chemung canal and feeder, or allowing his tows or rafts to be locked into said feeder.

Legislative Action:

Senate Journal, 1866. Petition presented and referred to the committee on claims, 52. Reported adversely. Laid on the table, 179. Recommitted to the committee on claims, 575. Reported by bill and referred to the committee of the whole, 666. Ordered to a third reading, 740. Bill lost, 817. Motion made to reconsider and laid on the table, 817. Motion taken from the table. Bill reconsidered and passed, 880. Motion to reconsider lost, 881. (See Senate document, No. 34, 1866.)

Assembly Journal, 1866. Bill received and referred to the committee on claims, 1551. Reported favorably and committed to the committee of the whole, 1597. Ordered to a third reading, 1660. Bill passed, 1725.

Award:

Under this act the Canal Board allowed the sum of $24,000.

Charles J. De Graw.

(Assignee of Albert G. Sage.)

Nature of Claim:

Compensation for loss sustained on contract, in consequence of the sliding of the canal bank, at the head of Moses Kill lock, Champlain canal, May, 1867.

Legislative Action:

Senate Journal, 1869. Bill introduced and referred to the committee on claims, 582. Assembly bill received, 682.

Reported favorably and committed to the committee of the whole, 821. Ordered to a third reading, 927. Bill lost, 971. Reconsidered and passed, 972.

Assembly Journal, 1869. Bill introduced and referred to the committee on claims, 146. Reported favorably and committed to the committee of the whole, 253. (See Assembly document, 537.) Ordered to a third reading, 414. Bill lost, 656. Reconsidered and passed, 1206. (See Laws of 1869, chapter 663.)

Under this act the Canal Board have allowed the sum of $21,530.37.

H. V. Delong.

(See Linus R. Clark and others.)

Ashael P. Dewey.

(See John C. Blaisdell and others.)

C. Dewey.

(See Linus R. Clark and others.)

John G. Deyer.

(See Linus R. Clark and others.)

Horace Dibble.

(See Erskine G. Clark and others.)

Elizabeth Dickerman.

Nature of Claim:

Compensation for damages to her premises in Olean, Cattaraugus county, by reason of a leak in the Genesee Valley canal, which flooded said premises with water.

Legislative Action:

Senate Journal, 1868. Bill introduced and referred to the committee on claims, 334.

Elizabeth Dickinson.

Nature of Claim:

Papers not found on file, and nature of the claim not known.

Legislative Action:

Senate Journal, 1868. Petition presented and referred to the committee on claims, 230.

George Dinsmore.

Nature of Claim:

Extra compensation upon contract to build Becker's lock, on the Champlain canal.

Legislative Action:

Senate Journal, 1870. Bill introduced and referred to the committee on claims, 110. Reported favorably and committed to the committee of whole, 348. Ordered to a third reading, 486. Bill passed, 498.

Assembly Journal, 1870. Senate bill received and referred to the committee on claims, 745. Reported favorably and referred to the committee of the whole, 788. Ordered to a third reading, 828. Bill passed, 868. (See Laws of 1870, chapter 160.)

Under this act the sum of $7,493.49 was allowed.

Charles A. Donaldson.

Nature of Claim:

Petitioner, a contractor for keeping in repair section No. 2, Erie canal, asks for $5,000 extra compensation for his services in repairing a break on the Four mile level, June 15, 1866.

Legislative Action:

Senate Journal, 1867. Petition presented and referred to the committee on claims, 99.

Samuel Donaldson.

Nature of Claim:

Compensation for extra work, as repair contractor of section No. 2, Erie canal, caused by extraordinary storms and an insufficient culvert.

Legislative Action:

Senate Journal, 1870. Petition presented and referred to the committee on claims, 37. Reported favorably and committed to the committee of the whole, 231. Ordered to a third reading, 331. Recommitted to the committee on claims, 340. Reported complete, with amendments, and ordered to a third reading, 602. Bill passed, 906. (See Senate document, No. 52, of 1870.)

Assembly Journal, 1870. Senate bill received and referred to the committee on claims, 1564. Reported favorably and committed to the committee of the whole, 1638. Ordered to a third reading, 1695. Bill passed, 1850. (See Laws of 1870, chapter 574.)

Under this act no award has yet been made.

P. O. Dougherty.

(See Linus R. Clark and others.)

George F. Dudley.

(See John C. Blaisdell and others.)

Margrette Dunn.

Nature of Claim:

Compensation for damages sustained by her in consequence of the State building an iron bridge over the Chenango canal, in the village of Hamilton.

Legislative Action:

Senate Journal, 1870. Petition presented and referred to the committee on claims, 122. Reported favorably and committed to the committee of the whole, 289. Ordered to a third reading, 409. Bill passed, 423.

Assembly Journal, 1870. Senate bill received and referred to the committee on claims, 630. Reported favorably and committed to the committee of the whole, 979. Ordered to a third reading, 1493.

J. A. and W. J. Dunham.

Nature of Claim:

Compensation for damages to their woolen works, by reason of the diversion of the waters of Limestone creek and Butternut creek, for canal purposes, in 1861.

Legislative Action:

Senate Journal, 1867. Petition presented and referred to the committee on claims, 81.

Andrew Dygert.

Nature of Claim:

Compensation for damages to his premises, in the village of Canajoharie, caused by the leakage of the Erie canal.

Legislative Action:

Senate Journal, 1870, Petition presented and referred to the committee on claims, 237. Bill introduced and referred to the committee on claims, 241. Reported favorably and committed to the committee of the whole, 487. Ordered to a third reading, 766. Bill passed, 868.

Assembly Journal, 1870. Senate bill received and referred to the committee on claims, 1478. Reported favorably and committed to the committee of the whole, 1638.

Lewis H. Eaton.

(See Joseph A. Scoville.)

Edward H. Edwards.

Nature of Claim:

For moneys alleged to have been wrongfully withheld from him by the superintendent and officers in charge of the Black River canal, and paid by them for unnecessary work in building a new bridge over said canal, in Dominick street, village of Rome, and for bottoming out said canal far below the level thereof.

Legislative Action:

Senate Journal, 1869. Petition presented and referred to the committee on claims, 341. Committee reported by bill. Committed to the committee of the whole, 582. Ordered to a third reading, 683. Bill passed, 699.

Assembly Journal, 1869. Bill received and referred to the committee on claims, 1373. Reported favorably and committed to the committee of the whole, 1415. Ordered to a third reading, 1797. Bill passed, 203. (See Laws of 1869, chapter 792.)

Under this act the Canal Board decided that the petitioner was not entitled to any award.

John Edwards.

Nature of Claim:

Compensation for loss of his horses, killed in crossing a bridge over the branch canal or side cut running from Higginsville to Oneida lake, at Higginsville, through defective condition of said bridge.

Legislative Action:

Senate Journal, 1868. Petition presented and referred to the committee on claims, 54. Reported favorably by bill, and committed to the committee of the whole, 327. Ordered to a third reading, 841. Bill passed, 851. (See Senate document No. 64, of 1868.)

Assembly Journal, 1868. Bill received and referred to the committee on claims, 1412. Reported favorably and committed to the committee of the whole, 1572.

Senate Journal, 1869. Resolution sent to the Assembly, requesting the transmission of papers, 34. Resolution that the papers be taken from the files and referred to the committee on claims, 54, 180. Committee reported by bill, which was committed to the committee of the whole, 212. Ordered to a third reading, 422. Bill passed, 437.

Assembly Journal, 1869. Bill received and referred to the committee on claims, 840. Committee reported favorably, 1415. Ordered to a third reading, 1796. Bill passed, 1958. (See laws of 1869, chapter 725.) Amount claimed, $377.40.

Under this act the canal appraisers have allowed the sum of $352.40.

George B. Efner.

Nature of Claim:

Compensation for loss of two horses, drowned in Erie canal, at Buffalo, December 24, 1868, in consequence of there being no bridge or guard at the junction of the street and canal.

Legislative Action:

Senate Journal, 1869. Petition presented and referred to the committee on claims, 158. Committee reported adversely. Report agreed to, 264. (See Senate document No. 54, of 1869.)

Rufus Eldred.

Nature of Claim:

Compensation for damages sustained by reason of the failure of the State to rebuild bridge over Oneida lake feeder, on the lands of petitioner.

Legislative Action:

Senate Journal, 1867. Bill introduced and referred to the committee on claims, 242.

Griffith Evans and Company.

(See Linus R. Clark and others.)

George H. Failing.

(See Linus R. Clark and others.)

John D. Fay and William Hollister.

Nature of Claim:

Compensation for the loss of yard, lumber and business, in consequence of the incapacity of the aqueduct at Rochester, during the flood of March, 1865.

Legislative Action:

Senate Journal, 1870. Bill introduced and referred to the committee on claims, 60. Reported favorably and committed to the committee of the whole, 436. Ordered to a third reading, 593. Bill passed, 622.

Assembly Journal, 1870. Senate bill received and referred to the committee on claims, 1079. Reported favorably and referred to the committee of the whole, 1109. Ordered to a third reading, 1494.

Benjamin Ferris.

(See Erskine G. Clark and others.)

Fifty-fifth Regiment, National Guard.

Nature of Claim:

Compensation for moneys advanced and uniforms and equipments worn out and lost during the late war, while in the service of the United States.

Legislative Action:

Senate Journal, 1869. Bill introduced and referred to the committee on claims, 299.

This bill was introduced in the Assembly in 1870 and became a law. (See chap. 673, Laws of 1870.) Under this act there was appropriated $15,028.36.

Fink's Basin Bridge.

Nature of Claim:

Compensation to the towns of Manheim, Danube and Little Falls, for loss of bridge over Mohawk river, March 17, 1868, in consequence of ice being retained by heavy flush plank on Rocky Rift dam.

Legislative Action:

Senate Journal, 1868. Petition presented and referred to the committee on claims, 373. Reported by bill. Referred to the committee of the whole, 611. Ordered to a third reading, 841. Bill passed, 852.

Assembly Journal, 1868. Bill received and referred to the committee on internal affairs of towns and counties, 1412. Reported favorably and committed to the committee of the whole, 1450. Ordered to a third reading, 1487. Bill passed, 1692. (See Laws of 1868, chapter 888.)

Under this act no award has yet been made.

John M. Fisk.

(See Linus R. Clark and others.)

Charles P. Fitch and Nelson Fitch.

(See Edward Mynders and others.)

D. H. Fitzhugh and Craig W. Wadsworth.

Nature of Claim :

Compensation for lands taken in the construction of the Genesee Valley canal, in the county of Livingston.

Legislative Action :

Senate Journal, 1868. Resolution sent to the Assembly requesting papers on file, and that the same be referred to the committee on canals, 75.

John Fitzpatrick.

(Assignee of Bernardus Swartwout.)

Nature of Claim :

Compensation for work done and materials furnished on section thirteen of the Cayuga and Seneca canal.

Legislative Action:

Senate Journal, 1868. Bill introduced and referred to committee on claims, 306. Reported favorably and committed to the committee of the whole, 337.

Senate Journal, 1869. Bill introduced and referred to the committee on claims, 85. Assembly bill received, 209. Reported favorably and committed to the committee of the whole, 222. Recommitted to the committee on claims, 223. Reported favorably and committed to the committee of the whole, 256. Ordered to a third reading, 445. Bill passed, 478.

Assembly Journal, 1869. Bill introduced and referred to committee on claims, 70. Reported favorably and committed to the committee of the whole, 212. Ordered to a third reading, 276. Bill passed, 341. (See Laws of 1869, chapter 139.)

Under this act the Canal Board has allowed the sum of $7,629.77.

John Fitzpatrick.

(Assignee of Bernardus Swartwout.)

Nature of Claim:

Compensation for work done and materials furnished on section thirteen of the Cayuga and Seneca canal, for which no estimate was made by the engineer in charge.

Legislative Action:

Senate Journal, 1870. Bill introduced and referred to the committee on claims, 43. Reported favorably and committed to the committee of the whole, 88. Ordered to a third reading, 136. Bill passed, 139.

Assembly Journal, 1870. Senate bill received and referred to the committee on claims, 229. Reported favorably and committed to the committee of the whole, 437. Ordered to third reading, 827. Bill passed, 867. Vetoed by the Governor. (See Senate Journal, 625.)

Another bill was subsequently introduced in the Senate, passed both Houses, and became a law. (See chapter 415 of Laws of 1870.)

Under this act no award has yet been made.

Elizabeth Flint.

(See B. H. Clark and others.)

Jeremiah Flood.

Nature of Claim:

Compensation for injuries to his horses, carriage and harness, in consequence of falling over the high embankment of the Erie canal, near Cohoes, in October, 1867.

Legislative Action:

Senate Journal, 1868. A petition in this matter was referred to the committee on claims. Reported adversely and report agreed to, 337. Petition in reference to claim presented and referred to the committee on claims, 543. (See Senate document No. 63, of 1868.)

A bill for the relief of the claimant was introduced in the Assembly in 1870, and passed both Houses, but was not signed by the Governor, jurisdiction having been conferred upon the Canal Appraisers to hear such cases, by general law. (See chapter 321, Laws of 1870.)

Forest Port Lumber and Stave Company.

(See Linus R. Clark and others.)

Fort Hunter Suspension Bridge Company.

Nature of Claim:

Compensation for damages to said bridge, by collision of boats escaping from Erie canal, during the freshet of March 17th, 1865.

Legislative Action:

Senate Journal, 1866. Petition presented and referred to the committee on claims, 171.

L. Jane B. Fowler.

(See J. J. Burton and others.)

Charles E. Frasier.

Nature of Claim:

Compensation for damages to the lands of claimant, caused by raising the Duta dam, in constructing the Duta feeder, of Black river canal.

Legislative Action:

Senate Journal, 1870. Petition presented and referred to the committee on claims, 41. Assembly bill received and referred to the committee on claims, 656. Reported favorably and referred to the committee of the whole, 745. Ordered to a third reading, 809. Bill passed, 938.

Assembly Journal, 1870. Petition presented and referred to the committee on claims, 89. Reported favorably and committed to the committee of the whole, 447. Ordered to a third reading, 827. Bill passed, 1030.

This bill was not signed by the Governor, jurisdiction having been conferred upon the Canal Appraisers, by general law. (See chapter 321 of Laws of 1870.)

Charles G. Frink.

Nature of Claim:

Compensation for damages sustained by reason of the leakage of the Erie canal, at West Troy, into the basement of the malt house owned by Patrick Rogers and occupied by said Frink.

Legislative Action:

Senate Journal, 1870. Bill introduced and referred to the committee on claims, 147. Reported favorably and committed to the committee of the whole, 689. Ordered to a third reading, 809. Bill passed, 871.

Assembly Journal, 1870. Senate bill received and referred to the committee on claims, 1478. Reported favorably and committed to the committee of the whole, 1638.

William Fritz.

(See Giles Shell and others.)

A. Frost.

(See Linus R. Clark and others.)

William S. Fullerton.

(See Enos C. Brooks.)

Fultonville and Johnstown Plank-road Company.

Nature of Claim:

Compensation for damages to the company's bridge over the Mohawk river, by a collision of boats escaping from the Erie canal, during the freshet of March 17, 1865.

Legislative Action:

Senate Journal, 1866. Petition presented and referred to the committee on roads and bridges, 176. Committee discharged and the matter referred to the committee on claims, 202.

Charles H. Gage and James H. Gage.

Nature of Claim:

Papers not found on file, and nature of claim not known.

Legislative Action:

Senate Journal, 1868. Petition presented and referred to the committee on claims, 244.

Thomas Gale, assignee of Charles J. DeGraw.

Nature of Claim:

For extra compensation upon contract for constructing the Oswego Falls dam, on the Oswego river, and upon a contract for constructing section No. 20, Chenango canal extension.

Legislative Action:

Senate Journal, 1870. Petition presented and referred to the committee on claims, 376. Bill introduced and referred to the committee on claims, 400. Assembly bill received and referred to the committee on claims, 655. Reported favorably and committed to the committee of the whole, 689. Ordered to a third reading, 809. Bill passed, 873.

Assembly Journal, 1870. Petition presented and referred to the committee on claims, 481. Reported favorably by bill (See Assembly document, No. 176) and committed to the committee of the whole, 814. Ordered to a third reading, 829. Bill passed, 1041. (See Laws of 1870, chapter 580.)

Under this act the Canal Board have allowed the sum of $25,997.73.

Thomas Gale and others.

(Liverpool Coarse Salt Company.)

Nature of Claim:

Compensation for damages in flooding their salt works in the town of Salina, through the enlargement of the Oswego canal and changing the bed of Bloody brook.

(See L. T. Hawley, President Liverpool Salt Company.)

James Gallagher.

Nature of Claims:

Compensation for damages sustained by him, caused by falling into the Erie canal, at Rochester, from neglect of State.

Legislative Action:

Senate Journal, 1866. Petition presented and referred to the committee on claims, 204. Committee reported adversely. Report agreed to, 1044.

Senate Journal, 1867. Petition taken from the files and referred to the committee on claims, 81.

This claim was introduced in the Assembly in 1868, passed both Houses and became a law.

Amount claimed, $23,925.

Award:

Under this act the Canal Appraisers have allowed the sum of $9,000.

Thomas Gallagher.

(See Erskine G. Clark and others.)

Edward Gay.

(See Erskine G. Clark and others.)

Gillett and Clark.

(See Linus R. Clark and others.)

Lucius Gills.

(See Linus R. Clark and others.)

Thomas Gilson.

Nature of Claim:

Compensation for extra services as clerk of Clinton prison.

Legislative Action:

Senate Journal, 1867. Petition presented and referred to the committee on finance, 76.

E. G. Gilson.

(See E. D. Sherwood and others.)

Joseph J. Glass.

(See Theodocia Wall and others.)

L. Goodwill.

(See Laura A. Poole and others.)

John Gordon.

Nature of Claim:

Compensation for removing and rebuilding a fence on his lands, along the Erie canal, in the town of Arcadia, in 1857.

Legislative Action:

Senate Journal, 1866. Papers taken from the files and referred to the committee on claims, 31. Committee reported adversely. Report laid on the table, 179. (See Senate document, No. 35, 1866.)

John Gordon.

Nature of Claim:

Compensation for labor and materials furnished in the completion of the Erie canal, in Wayne county.

Legislative Action:

Senate Journal, 1867. Papers taken from the files and referred to the committee on claims, 74. A majority of the committee reported favorably and by bill, 301. Minority reported adversely. (See Senate document, No. 17.) Bill ordered to a third reading, 494. Bill passed, 529.

Assembly Journal, 1867. Bill received and referred to the committee on claims, 975. Committee reported favorably, 1042. (See Assembly document, No. 17.) Ordered to a third reading, 1631. Bill passed, 1744.

This bill directs the Treasurer to pay on the warrant of the Comptroller to said John Gordon, his heirs or assignees, the sum of $122.69. (See Laws of 1867, chapter 609.)

Under this act the Treasurer has paid to the petitioner the sum of $122.69.

Frederick Gosskoff.

(See Giles Shell and others.)

William Goundrill.

(See Linus R. Clark and others.)

Philip Graff.

(See Linus R. Clark and others.)

John Graham.

(See John C. Blaisdell and others.)

Patrick Grattan and others.

John Riley and the heirs-at-law of Edward Murray, deceased.

Nature of Claim:

Compensation for constructing three locks on the Champlain canal at Fort Ann.

Legislative Action:

Senate Journal, 1870. Bill introduced and referred to the committee on claims, 76. Reported favorably and committed to committee of the whole, 391. Ordered to a third reading, 526. Bill passed, 539.

Assembly Journal, 1870. Senate bill received and referred to the committee on claims, 805. Reported favorably and committed to the committee of the whole, 979. Ordered to a third reading, 1492. Bill passed, 1753.

This bill was not signed by the Governor, jurisdiction having been conferred upon the Canal Appraisers, by general law. (See chapter 321, Laws of 1870.)

Martin Greene.

(See E. D. Sherwood and others.)

Job Green, Jr.

(See Louisa R. Pettit.)

Thomas Greenwood.

(See Ovid Plumb and others.)

Shimuel Griffin.

(See John C. Blaisdell and others.)

Daniel Guarin.

(See Erskine G. Clark and others.)

James Guarin.

(See Erskine G. Clark and others.)

Ellen A. Gutches.

(See Charles Carman.)

Solomon Hadcock.

(See Linus R. Clark and others.)

Sarah Haight.

Nature of Claim:

Extra compensation to Haight and Butler, as contractors, for building culverts over Erie canal, from section 141 to section 149, by reason of a change in the plan and the compulsion of the engineer in charge.

Legislative Action:

Senate Journal, 1867. Petition presented and referred to the committee on claims, 140.

Hall and Maltby.

(See Linus R. Clark and others.)

Charles Hall.

(See Ovid Plumb and others.)

George Halley.
(See John C. Blaisdell and others.)

Charles Hammond.
(See Linus R. Clark and others.)

W. C. Hanchett.
(See Linus R. Clark and others.)

Hanchett and Delong.
(See Linus R. Clark and others.)

Byron M. Hanks.
(See Lewis Selye, assignee.)

Samuel H. Harden.
(See John C. Blaisdell and others.)

Joseph H. Harris.
(See Erskine G. Clark and others.)

T. Franklin Harris.

(See Joseph J. Burton and others.)

Amasa P. Hart.

(See Theodocia Wall and others.)

John Harvey and the Personal Representatives of Walter Bissell, deceased.

Nature of Claim:

Compensation for damages in loss of logs and timber, during the freshet of May, 1865, in consequence of not being allowed to enter Chemung canal feeder.

Legislative Action:

Senate Journal, 1869. Bill introduced and referred to the committee on claims, 306. Reported favorably and committed to the committee of the whole, 372. Ordered to a third reading, 563. Bill passed, 589.

Assembly Journal, 1869. Bill received. Reported favorably (see Assembly document No. 164), and committed to the committee of the whole, 786. Bill ordered to a third reading and passed, 1639. (See Laws of 1869, chapter 466.)

Amount claimed, $8,078.50.

Award:

Under this act the Canal Appraisers allowed the sum of $10,518.70.

L. T. Hawley.

(President Liverpool Coarse Salt Company.)

Nature of Claims:

Compensation for damages resulting from the incapacity of the culvert on Bloody Brook, in the enlargement of the Oswego canal.

Legislative Action:

Senate Journal, 1867. Petition presented and referred to the committee on claims, 315.

John W. Hawn.

Nature of Claim:

Compensation for damages to the lands of claimant, by reason of the leakage of the Rocky Rift feeder, in the town of Minden, Montgomery county.

Legislative Action:

Senate Journal, 1868. Petition presented and referred to the committee on claims, 87.

Charles J. Hayden.

Nature of Claim:

Additional compensation as contractor for repairs of superintendents' section, No. 9, Erie canal; extra labor for repairs on said section being required by the flood of March 17, 1865.

Legislative Action:

Senate Journal, 1866. Petition presented and referred to the committee on claims, 521.

Mary Henry.

(See Erskine G. Clark and others.)

John G. Henry.

(See Erskine G. Clark and others.)

William Henry.

(See Erskine G. Clark and others.

George Herford.

(See Erskine G. Clark and others.)

Jeremiah Hern.

Nature of Claim:

Compensation for injuries sustained by falling from a canal bridge.

Legislative Action:

Senate Journal, 1868. Petition presented and referred to the committee on claims, 177.

Solomon Hess, Executor of John Hess, deceased.

Nature of Claim:

Compensation for lands taken in the enlargement of the Erie canal, and for other damages caused thereby.

Legislative Action:

Senate Journal, 1870. Petition presented and referred to the committee on claims, 106. Committee reported favorably and by bill. Committed to the committee of the whole, 218. Ordered to a third reading, 330. Bill passed, 338. (See Senate document No. 53, of 1870.)

Assembly Journal, 1870. Senate bill received and referred to the committee on judiciary. Judiciary committee discharged, and the bill referred to the committee on claims, 784. Reported favorably and committed to the committee of the whole, 814. Ordered to a third reading, 830. Bill passed, 939. (See Laws of 1870, chapter 161.)

Under this act no award has yet been made.

Hoard Spinn Company.

(See Linus R. Clark and others.)

Pitt Hoard.

(See Linus R. Clark and others.)

Charles B. Hoar.

(See Linus R. Clark and others.)

Gotlieb Hoffman.

(See Ovid Plumb and others.)

Edwin P. Hopkins.

(See Theodocia Wall and others.)

Amariah Holbrook and George B. Sherrill.

Nature of Claim:

Extra compensation for work done on the Champlain canal in building lock at Fort Edward.

Legislative Action:

Senate Journal, 1866. Petition presented and referred to the committee on claims, 139. Committee reported by bill, 205. Ordered to a third reading, 287. Bill passed, 330. (See Senate document, No. 37, 1866.)

Assembly Journal, 1866. Bill received and referred to the committee on claims, 314. Reported favorably, and referred to the committee of the whole, 771. Ordered to a third reading, 1420. Bill passed, 1520.

Award:

Under this act the Canal Board have allowed the sum of $7,533.83.

William Hollister.

(See John D. Fay.)

A. S. Hope.

Nature of Claim:

Compensation for damages to the starch factory of petitioner, situated in the city of Rochester, caused by the building of a bridge over the Erie canal on Hamilton street in said city.

Legislative Action:

Senate Journal, 1866. Petition presented and referred to the committee on claims, 149. Bill introduced and referred to the committee on claims, 269. Petition presented and referred to the committee on claims, 288.

John F. Hosch.

(Assignee of Samuel F. Case.)

Nature of Claim:

Extra compensation, as contractor, for keeping in repair section No. 4, Erie canal, and repairing the breaks and other damages caused by the flood of March, 1865.

Legislative Action:

Senate Journal, 1869. Petition presented and referred to the committee on claims, 51. Bill introduced and referred to the committee on claims, 53. Committee reported adversely. Question of agreeing thereto laid on the table, 423. Report of committee disagreed to and bill committed to the committee of the whole, 899. Report of the committee of the whole disagreed to, 928. Motion to reconsider laid on the table, 929. Motion to disagree with the report of the committee and order bill to third reading lost, 1036.

Senate Journal, 1870. Papers taken from the files and referred to the committee on claims, 49. Committee reported favorably in writing and by bill. Committed to the committee of the whole, 342. Ordered to a third reading, 766. Bill passed, 865. (See Senate document, No. 63, of 1870.)

Assembly Journal, 1870. Senate bill received and referred to the committee on claims, 1479. Reported favorably and committed to the committee of the whole, 1521. Ordered to a third reading, 1634. Bill passed, 1764. (See Laws of 1870, chapter 493.)

The sum awarded under this act shall not exceed five thousand dollars.

Under this act no award has yet been made by the Canal Board.

B. F. Hotckiss and Son.

(See Linus R. Clark and others.)

Edwin W. Howell.

(See Ovid Plumb and others.)

Augustus Howland.

(See Edward Mynders and others.)

David Hubbard.

(See Theodocia Wall and others.)

Thomas Hudson.

(See Linus R. Clark and others.)

Ephraim P. Huestis.

(See John C. Blaisdell and others.)

William Huggins.

(See Z. W. Barrett.)

John M. Humphrey.

Nature of Claim:

For repayment of the sum of $444.90, paid for lands to which the State had no title.

Legislative Action:

Senate Journal, 1868. Petition presented and referred to the committee on claims, 190. Reported favorably and committed to the committee of the whole, 318. Ordered to a third reading, 473. Bill passed, 478.

Assembly Journal, 1870. Senate bill received and referred to the committee of ways and means, 721. Reported favorably and committed to the committee of the whole, 907. Ordered to third reading. Bill passed, 1631.

This bill was vetoed by the Governor.

John Hunt and John Hunt, Jr.

(See Orrin W. Rose and others.)

Lewis B. Hurlburt.

(See Richard Reed and others.)

George S. Ingalls.

(See John C. Blaisdell and others.)

Daniel C. Jacobs.

(See Giles Shell and others.)

Henry G. Jackson and William Mudgett.

Nature of Claim:

Extra compensation for work done and material furnished as contractors on sections Nos. 4, 5 and 6 of the Chenango canal extension.

Legislative Action:

Senate Journal, 1870. Petition presented and referred to the committee on claims, 237. Bill introduced and referred to the committee on claims, 284. Reported favorably and committed to the committee of the whole, 436. Ordered to a third reading, 613. Bill passed, 636.

Assembly Journal, 1870. Senate bill received and referred to the committee on claims, 1080. Reported favorably and committed to the committee of the whole, 1109. Ordered to a third reading, 1494. Bill passed, 1725. (See Laws of 1870, chapter 575.)

The final award in this case has not yet been made.

Jefferson Johnson.

(See Orrin W. Rose and others.)

Jefferson Johnson.

(See Lucien Billinghurst and others.)

Robert R. Jones.

(See J. J. Burton and others.)

James Johnson.

(See Erskine G. Clark and others.)

Isaac Kelly.

(See Ovid Plumb and others.)

V. T. Kimball.

(See Linus R. Clark and others.)

Alexander Kincaid.

(See John C. Blaisdell and others.)

John Kingsbury, deceased (Heirs of).

(See Ovid Plumb and others.)

Johanna W. Kirchner and Thomas P. Richards.

Nature of Claim :

Compensation for damages to lands of claimant caused by the leakage of the Erie canal at West Troy.

Legislative Action :

Senate Journal, 1866. Petition presented and referred to the committee on claims, 106, 119. Committee reported adversely. Report agreed to, 1044.

Senate Journal, 1868. Papers taken from files and referred to the committee on claims, 368. Committee reported favorably and by bill. Referred to the committee of the whole, 600.

Senate Journal, 1870. Papers taken from the files and referred to the committee on claims, 152.

A. Kissam and Son.

Nature of Claim:

Compensation for loss of the canal boat "Nubia," sunk in the Erie canal November, 1868, and destroyed by the canal authorities to open the channel of said canal.

Legislative Action:

Senate Journal, 1870. Petition presented and referred to the committee on claims, 78. Adverse report, agreed to, 335. (See Senate document, No. 64, of 1870.)

Erastus Knapp.

(See Orrin W. Rose and others.)

Erastus Knapp.

(See Lucien Billinghurst and others.

Knowlton Brothers.

(See Linus R. Clark and others.)

Knowlton and Brothers.

Nature of Claim:

Papers not found on file and nature of claim not known.

Legislative Action:

Senate Journal, 1869. Petition presented and referred to the committee on claims, 818.

William Krall.

(See Giles Shell and others.)

Robert Lamb.

(See Linus R. Clark and others.)

E. D. Larkin.

(See E. D. Sherwood and others.)

Peter Lawson.

(See Erskine G. Clark and others.)

Jonathan D. Ledyard.

(See Gerrit Smith and others.)

Thomas R. Leet.

Nature of Claim:

Compensation for damages to the lands of claimant caused by the defective condition of the embankment of the Genesee Valley canal, and change of channel of Genesee river.

Legislative Action:

Senate Journal, 1870. Petition presented and referred to the committee on claims, 237. Bill introduced and referred to the committee on claims, 241. Reported favorably and committed to the committee of the whole, 487. Ordered to a third reading, 766. Bill passed, 867.

Assembly Journal, 1870. Senate bill received and referred to the committee on claims, to report complete, 1479. Reported complete and ordered to a third reading, 1521.

Limestone Creek (Owners of Lands on).

Nature of Claim:

Papers not found on file, and nature of claim not known.

Legislative Action:

Senate Journal, 1870. Bill introduced and referred to the committee on claims, 428.

Andrew W. Linclon, Josiah K. Lincoln and Charlton U. Lincoln.

Nature of Claim:

Compensation for damages to their mill property in the town of Perrinton, Monroe county, caused by a sudden and extraordinary discharge of water from the Erie canal.

Legislative Action:

Senate Journal, 1870. Bill introduced and referred to the committee on claims, 76. Reported favorably and committed to the committee of the whole, 417. Ordered to a third reading, 620. Bill passed, 639.

Assembly Journal, 1870. Senate bill received and referred to the committee on claims, 1079. Reported favorably and committed to the committee of the whole, 1109. Ordered to a third reading, 1494.

Liverpool Coarse Salt Company.

(See Thomas Gale and others.)

Little Falls. (Town of)

(See Fink's Basin Bridge.)

James S. Locke.

(See Ovid Plumb and others.)

A. Loomis.

Nature of Claim:

Compensation for damages caused by flooding his land by reason of the Rocky Rift dam, Mohawk river.

Legislative Action:

Senate Journal, 1866. Petition presented and referred to the committee on claims, 402. Reported favorably by bill and committed to the committee of the whole, 841.

Jarvis Lord.

(Assignee of James Bellows.)

Nature of Claim:

(See James Bellows.)

Legislative Action:

Senate Journal, 1866. Bill introduced and referred to the committee on claims, 583. Reported favorably and referred to the committee of the whole, 740. Ordered to a third reading, 752. Bill passed, 759.

Assembly Journal, 1866. Bill received and referred to the committee on claims, 1351. Reported favorably and referred to the committee of the whole, 1476. Ordered to a third reading, 1660. Bill passed, 1691.

Award:

Under this act the Canal Board allowed the sum of $30,000.

J. Lord.

(See Linus R. Clark and others.)

G. Lord.

(See Linus R. Clark and others.)

Lewis M. Loss.

(Attorney for William Mudgett.)

Nature of Claim:

Extra compensation for work done and materials furnished in constructing section No. 18 of the Chenango canal extension.

Legislative Action:

Senate Journal, 1870. Petition presented and referred to the committee on claims, 68. Bill introduced and referred to the committee on claims, 70. Reported favorably and committed to the committee of the whole, 154. Ordered to a third reading, 227. Bill passed, 270.

Assembly Journal, 1870. Senate bill received and referred to the committee on claims, 431. Reported favorably and committed to the committee of the whole, 510. Ordered to a third reading, 828. Bill passed, 863. (See Laws of 1870, chapter 148.)

Award:

The Canal Board have awarded to the petitioner the sum of $25,285.00.

Aaron Lovett.

Nature of Claim:

For payment of the certificate held by him as a soldier of the war of 1812.

Legislative Action:

Senate Journal, 1868. Petition presented and referred to the committee on finance, 142.

W. W. Lyon and W. R. Lyon.

(See J. J. Burton and others.)

Thomas Machan.

Nature of Claim:

Papers not found on file and nature of claim not known.

Legislative Action:

Senate Journal, 1870. Bill introduced and referred to the committee on claims, 147.

Manheim (Town of).

(See Fink's Basin Bridge.)

William Manning.

Nature of Claim:

Compensation for artillery harness, trimmings, etc., furnished to the State.

Legislative Action:

Senate Journal, 1866. Petition presented and referred to the committee on militia, 81. Bill introduced and referred to the same committee, 101. Committee reported adversely. Agreed to, and bill rejected, 179.

Walter W. Marsh.

(See Richard Reed and others.)

Russell Martin, Assignee of William McArthur.

Nature of Claim:

Compensation for work done and material furnished on repair section No. 3, Genesee Valley canal.

Legislative Action:

Senate Journal, 1868. Bill introduced and referred to committee on claims, 334. Reported favorably and committed to the committee of the whole, 388. Ordered to third reading, 612. Bill passed, 618.

Assembly Journal, 1868. Senate bill received and referred to committee on claims, 1006. Reported favorably and committed to the committee of the whole, 1043. Ordered to a third reading, 1365. Bill passed, 1457. (See Laws of 1868, chapter 494.)

Award:

Under this act the Canal Board allowed the sum of $7,469.54.

Russell Martin.

Nature of Claim:

Payment for building a dam in one of the feeders of the Genesee Valley canal, and for damages arising from the flood of March, 1865.

Legislative Action:

Senate Journal, 1866. Petition presented and referred to the committee on claims, 40. Bill received from Assembly and referred to the committee on claims, 709. Reported favorably and referred to the committee of the whole, 723. Ordered to a third reading, 830. Bill passed, 846.

Assembly Journal, 1866. Petition presented and referred to the committee on claims, 637. Reported favorably by bill and referred to the committee of the whole, 666. Ordered to a third reading, 1159. Passed, 1262. (See Laws of 1866, chapter 909.)

Award:

Under this act the Canal Board allowed the sum of $9,500

John P. Matteson.

(See Erskine G. Clark and others.)

Julia M. Maxwell.

(See Willis B. Sayre and others.)

Mary Ann McAnarney.

Nature of Claim:

Compensation for damages to her premises in the city of Rochester, in consequence of building a new bridge over the Erie canal, on Brown street, in said city.

Legislative Action:

Senate Journal, 1870. Petition presented and referred to the committee on claims, 376. Bill introduced and referred to the committee on claims, 377.

Archibald McArthur.

Nature of Claim:

Extra compensation as contractor for repairs on section No. 2, Black River canal, in consequence of the escape of the waters of the North Branch reservoir.

Legislative Action:

Senate Journal, 1870. Petition presented and referred to the committee on claims, 393. Reported favorably by bill and referred to the committee of the whole, 520. Ordered to a third reading, 808. Bill passed, 868.

Assembly Journal, 1870. Senate bill received and referred to the committee on claims, 1478. Reported favorably, and committed to the committee of the whole, 1638. Ordered to a third reading, 1695. Bill passed, 1846. (See Laws of 1870, chapter 751.)

Under this act no award has yet been made.

John McBurney and George B. Bradley.

Nature of Claim:

Compensation for damages caused by raising the embankment of the Chemung canal, at Corning.

Legislative Action:

Senate Journal, 1866. Petition presented and referred to the committee on claims, 254.

(See Geo. B. Bradley.)

Wm. McClary.

Nature of Claim:

Extra compensation on contract.

Legislative Action:

Senate Journal, 1866. Resolution requesting the Assembly to transmit the papers to the Senate, 243, 272. Papers received and referred to the committee on claims, 290.

Senate Journal, 1868. Papers taken from the files and referred to the committee on claims, 120.

Senate Journal, 1869. Papers taken from the files, and referred to the committee on claims, 147. Committee reported adversely, report agreed to, 341.

Daniel McGeary.

(See William W. Reed.)

Francis E. McHenry.

(See Willis B. Sayre and others.)

Francis E. McHenry.

(See Mathew Sayre, Heirs of.)

Patrick McIntyre.

(See Erskine G. Clark and others.)

Alexander McKee.

(See Erskine G. Clark and others.)

81

Mary McKeever.

(See L. Y. Avery.)

Mead and Graves.

(See Linus R. Clark and others.)

Elliott Meeker.

(See Ovid Plumb and others.)

Frederick Melcher.

(See Giles Shell and others.)

Edmund Merry.

(See Theodocia Wall and others.)

Militia Officers.

Nature of Claim:

Payment for the services of the chief and assistant enrolling officers, appointed by the Governor in 1862, to enroll the militia.

Legislative Action:

Senate Journal, 1866. Petition presented and referred to the committee on militia, 88.

A. C. Miller, Trustee of Port Leyden Iron Company.

(See Linus R. Clark and others.)

John Miller.

(See John C. Blaisdell and others.)

Nelson Miller.

(See Erskine G. Clark and others.)

Sidney B. Miller.

(See Erskine G. Clark and others.

Jeremiah F. Miller.

(See Erskine G. Clark and others.)

Christian Miller.

(See Giles Shell and others.)

Mary Ann Millis.

Nature of Claim:

Compensation for damages caused by the Oswego canal enlargement.

Legislative Action:

Senate Journal, 1869. Bill introduced and referred to the committee on claims, 599. Reported favorably and committed to the committee of the whole, 752. Ordered to a third reading, 926. Bill passed, 951.

Assembly Journal, 1869. Bill introduced and referred to the committee on claims, 111. Reported favorably in writing and committed to the committee of the whole, 836. (See Assembly document, No. 134, of 1869.) Ordered to a third reading, 1373. Bill passed, 1584. (See Laws of 1869, chapter 540.)

Amount claimed, $3,350.

Award:

Under this act the Canal Appraisers have allowed the sum of $3,825.

M. H. Mills.

(See C. A. Daniels.)

Michael Minton.

(See John C. Blaisdell and others.)

T. W. Moak.

(See Linus R. Clark and others.)

Joseph C. Moore.

(See John C. Blaisdell and others.)

S. Moore.

(See Linus R. Clark and others.)

Mortimer C. Mordoff.

(See B. H. Clark and others.)

Morgan and Ames.

(See Linus R. Clark and others.)

Samuel L. Mott.

Nature of Claim:

Compensation for damages to his saw-mill and shingle-machine, on Black river, caused by the diversion of the waters of said river for canal purposes.

Legislative Action:

Senate Journal, 1870. Petition presented and referred to the committee on claims, 376. Bill introduced and referred to the committee on canals. Committee discharged, and bill referred to the committee on claims, 749. Reported favorably, and committed to the committee of the whole, 767. Ordered to a third reading, 950.

Moulton, Herrick and Company.

(See Linus R. Clark and others.)

William Mudgett.

(See Henry G. Jackson and Lewis M. Loss.)

Joseph Muir.

(See Linus R. Clark and others.)

Michael Mulchy.

(See Linus R. Clark and others.)

John C. Munro.

(See E. D. Sherwood and others.)

David A. Munro.

(See E. D. Sherwood and others.)

Edward Murray, deceased (Heirs of).

(See Patrick Grattan and others.)

M. E. Murray.

(See Albert H. Pickard and others.)

Thomas Murray and James Quillinan.

Nature of Claim:

Compensation for personal injuries received by falling from a bridge over the Champlain canal.

Legislative Action:

Senate Journal, 1870. Petition presented and referred to the committee on claims, 56. Reported favorably by bill and committed to the committee of the whole, 363. Ordered to a third reading, 766. Bill passed, 865.

Assembly Journal, 1870. Senate bill received and referred to the committee on claims, 1478. Reported favorably and committed to the committee of the whole, 1638.

Hamilton Murray, deceased, legal Representatives of.

(See Gerrit Smith and others.)

Edward Mynders, Charles P. Fitch, Nelson Fitch, Augustus Howland and Charles N. Tuttle.

Nature of Claim:

Compensation for loss of lumber, etc., by fire, at Auburn prison.

Legislative Action:

Senate Journal, 1870. Petition presented and referred to the committee on claims, 180.

Robert Nichols, Jr.

(See John C. Blaisdell and others.)

John S. Nichols.

(See Linus R. Clark and others.)

William Nightingale.

(See E. D. Sherwood and others.)

Sophronia F. Ninde.

Nature of Claim:

Compensation for damages to the hydraulic canal wall of petitioner, in the village of Fulton, Oswego county, by a break in the berm bank of the Oswego canal.

Legislative Action:

Senate Journal, 1866. Petition presented and referred to the committee on claims, 29. Bill introduced and referred to the committee on claims, 32. Bill reported favorably with amendments, and referred to the committee of the whole, 134. Ordered to a third reading, 206. Bill passed, 217. (See Senate document No. 25, 1866.)

Assembly Journal, 1866. Bill received and referred to the committee on claims, 479. Committee reported favorably. Bill referred to the committee of the whole, 667. Ordered to a third reading, 1186. Bill passed, 1419.

Amount claimed $350.00

Award:

Under this act the Canal Appraisers have allowed the sum of $353.00.

Nine Mile Creek, Owners of Property on.

Nature of Claim:

Compensation for damages sustained in consequence of the break in the dam, at the foot of Otisco lake, Onondaga county, July, 1868.

Legislative Action:

Senate Journal, 1870. Bill introduced and referred to the committee on canals, 59. Committee discharged and bill referred to the committee on claims, 63. Reported favorably and committed to the committee of the whole, 88. Ordered to a third reading, 133. Bill passed, 139.

Assembly Journal, 1870. Senate bill received and referred to the committee on claims, 229. Reported favorably and referred to the committee of the whole, 399. Ordered to a third reading, 827. Bill passed, 866. (See Laws of 1870, chapter 164.)

[NOTE. The books of the Canal Appraisers do not designate the names of the claimants under this act. For claims and awards see Supplement.]

Reuben C. Oatman.

(See Erskine G. Clark and others.)

David Ogden.

Nature of Claim:

To refund to him certain taxes levied upon his lands by the State.

Legislative Action:

Senate Journal, 1866. Petition presented and referred to the committee on the judiciary, 149.

Charles Papke.

(See Giles Shell and others.)

E. W. Park.

Nature of Claim:

Papers not found on file and nature of claim unknown.

Legislative Action:

Senate Journal, 1868. Message from Assembly received, requesting that the papers on file be transmitted to the Assembly. Ordered accordingly, 69.

Andrew Parker.

(See Erskine G. Clark and others.)

Cornelius R. Parsons.

(See B. H. Clark and others.)

James Pattan.

(See E. D. Sherwood and others.)

Robert J. Peck.

(See Erskine G. Clark and others.)

William Petrie & Co.

Nature of Claim:

Compensation for damages to the canal boat "A. M. Hitchcock," and cargo of corn, sunk at Brighton lower lock, September 14, 1866.

Legislative Action:

Senate Journal, 1867. Petition presented and referred to the committee on claims, 130. Adverse report in writing. Agreed to, 612. (See Senate document No. 67, 1867.)

Louisa R. Pettit and Job Green, Jr.

Nature of Claim:

Compensation for damages to their lands, caused by the coffer dam between the Phenix dam and premises of claimants, and also by the Jack's Reef's improvement.

Legislative Action:

Senate Journal, 1869. Petition presented and referred to the committee on claims, 236. Bill introduced and referred to the same committee, 241. Reported favorably and committed to the committee of the whole, 372. Ordered to a third reading, 562. Bill passed, 588.

Assembly Journal, 1869, Bill received and referred to the committee on claims, 1153. Reported favorably and committed to the committee of the whole, 1415. Ordered to a third reading, 1796. Bill passed, 2011. (See Laws of 1869, chapter 764.)

Award:

Amount claimed, $2,500. Under this act the Canal Appraisers have allowed the sum of $2,945.29.

Albert H. Pickard and others.

Nature of Claim:

Compensation for damages to their land in the town of Amherst, Erie county, caused by raising the dam at the mouth of Tonawanda creek the water having overflowed and set back on about eighteen acres. Also taking about four acres for tow-paths, along border of said lands.

Legislative Action:

Senate Journal, 1866. Petition presented and referred to the committee on claims, 133. Bill introduced in the Assembly in 1869 and became a law. (See chapter 604, Laws of 1869.) For awards, see supplement.

Lucy Pickard, P. H. Pickard and L. A. Pickard.

(See Albert H. Pickard and others.)

Jacob Piron.

Nature of Claim:

Compensation for damages to his lands, caused by a break in the Erie canal at Pool's brook, Onondaga county, September 28, 1869.

Legislative Action:

Senate Journal, 1870. Petition presented and referred to the committee on claims, 42. Bill introduced and referred to the committee on claims, 44. Reported favorably and committed to the committee of the whole, 231. Ordered to a third reading, 331. Bill passed, 338.

Assembly Journal, 1870. Senate bill received and referred to the committee on claims, 521. Reported favorably and committed to the committee of the whole, 735. Ordered to a third reading, 829. Bill passed, 862. (See Laws of 1870, chapter 147.)

Under this act no award has yet been made by the appraisers.

George W. Phelps.

Nature of Claim:

Extra compensation as contractor for repairs on section No. 2, Genesee Valley canal.

Legislative Action:

Senate Journal, 1870. Petition presented and referred to the committee on claims, 267. Bill introduced and referred to the committee on claims, 278. Reported favorably and committed to the committee of the whole, 417. Ordered to a third reading, 766. Bill passed, 865.

Assembly Journal, 1870. Bill introduced and referred to the committee on claims, 590. Reported favorably, in writing (see Document 159), and committed to the committee of the whole, 788. Referred back to the committee. Reported complete and ordered to a third reading, 1678. Bill passed, 1765. (See Laws of 1870, chapter 494.)

Under this act no award has yet been made.

J. C. Platt.

(See E. D. Sherwood and others.)

Ovid Plumb and others.

Treman & Banks, James S. Locke, Stephen Williams, heirs of John Kingsbury, deceased ; John A. Starling, Augustus Botsford, Ellicott Meeker, Thomas C. Sleeper, Alonzo Banks, Gotlieb Hoffman, Edwin W. Howell, Edwin S. Rumsey, George Rumsey, Josiah A. Stearns, Mary J. Rhodes (administratrix of Joseph Rhodes, deceased), Isaac Kelly, Judah Whitcomb, Horace Seaman, Samuel Coe, William Dean and Charles C. Coston.

Nature of Claim:

Compensation for damages sustained by them in consequence of letting the waters of the Chemung canal into Catherine creek, by cutting out waste-weirs, and breaks, in June, 1857.

Legislative Action:

Senate Journal, 1867. Petition presented and referred to the committee on claims, 35.

Senate Journal, 1868. Message received from the Assembly, requesting the transmission of the papers in this case. Ordered accordingly, 109.

Senate Journal, 1869. Petition presented and referred to the committee on claims, 35. Committee reported in writing and by bill, 138. (See Senate document, No. 33, of 1869.) Ordered to third reading, 382. Bill passed, 398.

Assembly Journal, 1869. Bill received and referred to the committee on claims, 793. Reported favorably and committed to the committee of the whole, 1024. Ordered to a third reading, 1796. Bill passed, 2010. (See Laws of 1869, chapter 763.)

Under this act the Canal Appraisers have made the following awards:

	Amount claimed.	Amount allowed.
Ovid Plumb	$3,496 00	$3,187 50
Treman & Banks	3,136 74	3,196 40
James S. Locke	10,488 00	9,562 50
Stephen Williams	3,293 60	2,962 50
John Kingsbury, deceased (heirs of)	3,781 20	3,609 37
John A. Sterling	908 96	908 96
Augustus Botsford	2,176 26	2,066 55
Elliott Meeker	1,012 00	843 75
Thomas C. Sleeper	9,016 00	8,906 25
Alonzo Banks	5,163 40	5,170 40
Gottleib Hoffman	552 00	562 50
Edwin W. Howell	1,367 12	1,393 62
Edwin S. and George Rumsey	2,921 00	2,601 50
Josiah A. Stearns	3,192 40	3,065 62
Mary J. Rhodes (administratrix)	7,360 00	3,045 88
Isaac Kelly	759 92	616 87
Judah Whitcomb	3,772 00	3,231 25
Horace Seaman	2,816 20	2,718 75
Samuel Coe	1,610 00	1,345 31
William Dean	1,274 20	1,278 75
Charles C. Corton	1,318 36	1,307 46

Laura A. Poole, and others, L. Goodwill, Daniel Wagner and Andrew Wagner.

Nature of Claim:

Compensation for damage to their lands, caused by raising the waters of Seneca river, by means of the coffer dams between the Phenix dams and said lands, and by the Jack's Reefs improvement.

Legislative Action:

Senate Journal, 1870. Petition presented and referred to the committee on claims, 527. Bill introduced and referred to the committee on claims, 543.

Port Leyden Iron Company.

(See Linus R. Clark and others.)

Portable Steam Engine and M. Company.

(See Linus R. Clark and others.)

S. D. Porter.

(See Brackett H. Clark and others.)

Joseph Potvin.

(See Erskine G. Clark and others.)

L. S. Pratt.

(See Linus R. Clark and others.)

James Preslow.

(See E. D. Sherwood and others.)

Anthony Pulver.

Nature of Claim:

To refund taxes illegally collected on his real estate in the town of Ancram, Columbia county.

Legislative Action:

Senate Journal, 1869. Petition presented and referred to the committee on finance, 186.

Senate Journal, 1870. Petition presented and referred to the committee on claims.

George Quinn and Daniel Sharp.

Nature of Claim:

Petitioners claim compensation for losses received under "Stop Law," being obliged to abandon their contract, and cease labor on section No. 54 (Genesee Valley canal), commonly called "The Deep Cut."

Legislative Action:

Senate Journal, 1866. Petition presented and referred to committee on claims, 33.

John F. Ransom.

(See Linus R. Clark and others.)

Hezekiah L. Raymond.

Nature of Claim:

For repayment for building bridge in town of Neversink.

Legislative Action:

Senate Journal, 1866. Petition presented and referred to the committee on claims, 402. Committee discharged from further consideration of petition, 432. Referred to the committee on roads and bridges. Bill introduced in the Assembly in 1867 and became a law. (See chapter 187, Laws of 1867.)

Burton J. Reed.

Nature of Claim:

Petitioner desires a special act to appeal from decision of the Appraisers, who awarded him $1,752 for a portion of his land, appropriated in the construction of De Ruyter reservoir, the legal time for appeal having expired.

Legislative Action:

Senate Journal, 1866. Papers taken from the files and referred to committee on claims, 469.

Committee reported adversely. Agreed to, 966. (See Senate document No. 87, 1866.)

Wm. W. Reed and Daniel McGeary.

Nature of Claim:

Petitioners, who were contractors for section No. 1, Genesee Valley canal and section No. 2, Chenango canal, claim additional compensation, for extra labor performed in repairing the breaks in said sections, caused by the freshet of March, 1865.

Legislative Action:

Senate Journal, 1866. Petition presented and referred to the committee on claims, 106. Adverse report. Agreed to, 461. (See Senate document No. 61, 1866.)

Richard Reed, and others, Lewis B. Hurlburt, Peter Shea, Walter W. Marsh, John M. Swinerton and E. Benedict Strong.

Nature of Claim:

Compensation for damages to their lands, in the town of Perrinton, Monroe county, flooded by a break in Erie canal, November 25th, 1864.

Legislative Action:

Senate Journal, 1870. Bill introduced and referred to the committee on claims, 76. Reported favorably and committed to the committee of the whole, 436. Ordered to a third reading, 766. Bill passed, 866.

Assembly Journal, 1870. Reported favorably, 1634. Ordered to a third reading, 1637.

Charles Regel.

(See Giles Shell and others.)

Remington Paper Company.

(See Linus R. Clark and others.)

James G. Reynolds.

Nature of Claim:

Compensation for damages by reason of the diversion of water from petitioner's mill, situated on Braddock's dam, Oswego river, section No. 2.

Legislative Action:

Senate Journal, 1866. Petition presented and referred to the committee on claims, 88. Adverse report. Laid on table, 460. (See Senate document No. 63, 1866.)

Nathan Reynolds.

Nature of Claim:

Compensation for damages by reason of a waste-weir on Chemung canal, town of Big Flats.

Legislative Action:

Senate Journal, 1866. Petition presented and referred to the committee on claims, 43. Reported favorably by bill and referred to the committee of the whole, 247. Ordered to a third reading, 308. Bill passed, 317. (See Senate document No. 41, 1866.)

Assembly Journal, 1866. Bill received and referred to the committee on claims, 648. Reported favorably and referred to the committee of the whole, 1112. Ordered to a third reading, 1187. Bill passed, 1437.

Amount claimed, $1,000.

Award.

Under this act the Canal Appraisers have allowed the sum of $500.

Thomas P. Richards.

(See Johanna M. Kirchner.)

Mary J. Rhodes, Administratrix of Joseph Rhodes, deceased.

(See Ovid Plumb and others.)

Abram Richmond.

(See Eben B. Wait and others.)

Seth M. Richmond.

(See Eben B. Wait and others.)

John Riley.

(See Patrick Grattan and others.)

John Roberts.

(See Z. W. Barrett.)

Silas G. Roberts.

Nature of Claim:

Compensation for damages to the property of claimant, situated in the town of Nunda, Livingston county, caused by water flowing from the waste-weir of the Genesee Valley canal.

Legislative Action:

Senate Journal, 1868. Petition presented and referred to the committee on claims, 178. Reported favorably by bill and committed to the committee of the whole, 183.

John S. Roberts.

Nature of Claim:

Compensation for building and maintaining a bridge across the channel of the waste-weir of the Genesee Valley canal on lands of claimant in the town of Mount Morris, Livingston county, and compensation for damages to said lands.

[NOTE.—The above petition is on file. Claimant may be the John Roberts mentioned in claim of Z. W. Barrett.]

Mary Robertson and others.

Nature of Claim:

Indemnity for lands at Rouse's Point ceded to United States.

Legislative Action:

Senate Journal, 1869. Petition presented and referred to the committee on the judiciary, 236. Committee reported adversely, and question of agreeing to the report laid on the table, 424.

City of Rochester.

Nature of Claim:

Compensation for damages caused by the flow of water through the Genesee Valley canal and feeder, into the Erie canal, through the streets of said city, March, 1865.

Legislative Action:

Senate Journal, 1868. Bill introduced and referred to the committee on claims, 44. Reported favorably, in writing, and committed to the committee of the whole, 260. Ordered to a third reading, 436. Bill passed, 442. (See Senate document No. 55.)

Assembly Journal, 1868. Bill received and referred to the committee on affairs of cities, 756. Reported favorably and committed to the committee of the whole, 798. Ordered to a third reading, 849. Bill passed, 1254. (See Laws of 1868, chapter 342.)

Amount claimed, $19,964.43. Under this act no award has yet been made.

Orrin W. Rose, and others, Jefferson Johnston, John Hunt, John Hunt, Jr., Erastus Knap and George Rose.

Nature of Claims:

Compensation for damages for loss of logs carried away in consequence of a break in the Chemung canal feeder dam, March 17, 1865, in town of Corning, Steuben county.

Legislative Action:

Senate Journal, 1866. Petition presented and referred to the committee on claims, 288.

Same claim as Lucian Billinghurst and others.

Orrin W. Rose.

(See Lucien Billinghurst and others.)

George Rose.

(See Orrin W. Rose and others.)

S. B. Rowe.

(See E. D. Sherwood and others.)

George Rumsey.

(See Ovid Plumb and others.)

Edwin S. Rumsey.

(See Ovid Plumb and others.)

Albert G. Sage.

(See Charles J. De Graw.)

Charles Sahr.

(See Giles Shell and others.)

George W. Sauer.

Nature of Claim:

Compensation for damages sustained by him in loss of horses, and for other expenses, in the year 1861, incurred in equipping and perfecting a detachment of the Third regiment of cavalry, N. G. S. N. Y.

Legislative Action:

Senate Journal, 1868. Petition presented and referred to the committee on militia. Reported favorably by bill and committed to the committee of the whole, 612. Ordered to a third reading, 841. Bill passed, 852.

Assembly Journal, 1868. Bill introduced and referred to the committee on militia and public defense, 1056. Reported favorably and committed to the committee of the whole, 1119. Recommitted with power to report complete, 1148. Senate bill substituted and ordered to a third reading, 1412. Bill passed, 1581.

Under this act the Comptroller is directed to draw his warrant on the Treasurer for the sum of twenty-five hundred ($2,500) dollars for the payment of said claim. (Laws of 1868, chapter 861.)

Under this act the sum of two thousand five hundred dollars has been paid to the claimant.

George P. Saunders.

Nature of Claim:

Compensation for loss of canal boat "Mary M. Siver," in Erie canal, July, 1865.

Legislative Action:

Senate Journal, 1866. Petition presented and referred to the committee on claims, 31. Bill introduced and referred to the committee on claims, 34. Reported adversely. Report agreed to, 945. (See Senate document 93.)

Oney Sayles.

Nature of Claim:

Compensation for damages to three mills of the petitioner, situated on Butternut and Lime Stone creeks, Onondaga county, resulting from the diversion of the waters of said streams for canal purposes.

Legislative Action:

Senate Journal, 1867. Petition presented and referred to the committee on claims, 81.

James M. Sayre.

(See Willis B. Sayre and others.)

Willis B. Sayre and others.

Julia E. Maxwell, Eloisa O. Beebe, James M. Sayre, and Francis E. McHenry (heirs-at-law of Mathew Sayre, deceased).

Nature of Claim:

Compensation for damages caused by the leakage of the Chemung canal and feeder, in the town Horseheads, whereby about forty-five acres of valuable land was flooded.

Legislative Action:

Senate Journal, 1867. Bill introduced and referred to the committee on claims, 37. Reported favorably and committed to the committee of the whole, 1038.

Senate Journal, 1869. Petition presented and referred to the committee on claims, 80, 81. Committee reported in writing, and by bill (see Senate document, No. 40 of 1869), and committed to the committee of the whole, 160. Ordered to a third reading, 562. Bill passed, 588.

Assembly Journal, 1869. Bill received and referred to the committee on claims, 1153. Reported favorably, and committed to the committee of the whole, 1415.

Mathew Sayre (heirs of).

(See Willis B. Sayre and others.)

John Schafer.

Nature of Claim:

Compensation for damages caused by a break in the Erie canal. November, 1864.

Legislative Action:

Senate Journal, 1866. Petition presented, and referred to the committee on claims, 47.

Aaron Schuyler.

Nature of Claim:

Papers not found on file, and nature of the claim unknown.

Legislative Action:

Senate Journal, 1870. Papers taken from files, and referred to the committee on claims, 407.

Assembly Journal, 1870. Papers taken from files, and referred to the committee on claims, 775.

Joseph A. Scoville and Lewis H. Eaton (assignees of Myron Bangs).

Nature of Claim:

Extra compensation for keeping in repair superintendent's section No. 8, of the Erie canal.

Legislative Action:

Senate Journal, 1869. Bill introduced and referred to the committee on claims, 212. Committee reported adversely, and question of agreeing to report laid on the table, 341.

Senate Journal, 1870. Petition presented and referred to committee on claims, 112. Bill introduced and referred to the committee on claims, 113. Reported favorably and committed to the committee of the whole, 391. Ordered to a third reading, 527. Bill passed, 539.

Assembly Journal, 1870. Senate bill received and referred to the committee on claims, 805. Reported favorably and committed to the committee of the whole, 908. Ordered to a third reading, 1002. Bill passed, 1211. (See Laws of 1870, chapter 249.)

Under this act no award has yet been made.

Horace Seaman.

(See Ovid Plumb and others.)

Second Regiment, National Guard.

Nature of Claim:

Compensation for value of uniforms and equipments of members of said regiment at the time they enlisted and were mustered into the service of the United States, May 31, 1861; their uniforms, etc., being lost and worn out in said service.

Legislative Action:

Senate Journal, 1868. Petition presented and referred to the committee on finance, 668. Committee discharged and petition referred to the committee on militia, 679. Reported favorably by bill and referred to the committee of the whole, 738. Recommitted with power to report complete, 1053. Bill passed, 1058.

Assembly Journal, 1868. Bill received and ordered to a third reading, 1673. Bill lost, 1681. Motion to reconsider laid on the table, 1682. Motion to take from the table carried, 1709. Motion to reconsider the final vote lost, and the bill rejected, 1710.

Lewis Selye, assignee of Byron M. Hanks.

Nature of Claim:

Extra compensation for repairing damages to section No. 11, Erie canal, by the flood of March 17, 1865, of which section Byron M. Hanks was contractor.

Legislative Action:

Senate Journal, 1866. Petition presented and referred to the committee on claims. Reported favorably by bill and referred to the committee of the whole, 854. Ordered to a third reading, 928. Bill passed, 937.

Assembly Journal, 1866. Bill received and referred to the committee on claims, 1603. Reported favorably and referred to the committee of the whole, 1630. Ordered to a third reading, 1660. Passed, 1724.

Award:

Under this act the Canal Board have allowed the sum of $15,201.

Seneca Indians,

Nature of Claim:

Compensation for damages caused by raising the banks of the feeder on the Oil Spring reservation; supplying water to the Genesee Valley canal.

Legislative Action:

Senate Journal, 1869. Bill introduced and referred to the committee on claims, 289. Bill reported favorably and committed to the committee of the whole, 443. Ordered to a third reading, 563. Bill passed, 604.

Assembly Journal, 1869. Bill introduced and referred to the committee on Indian affairs, 562. Reported favorably and committed to the committee of the whole, 634. Senate bill received and referred to the committee on claims, 1180. Reported favorably and committed to the committee of the whole, 1415.

Henry I. Seymour.

Nature of Claim:

Compensation for damages to his chair manufactory, in West Troy; caused by the leakage of the Erie canal.

Legislative Action:

Senate Journal, 1869. Bill introduced and referred to the committee on claims, 83. Committee reported favorably. Ordered to a third reading, 562. Bill passed, 604.

Assembly Journal, 1869. Bill received and referred to the committee on claims, 1180. Committee reported adversely and report agreed to, 1415.

Senate Journal, 1870. Bill introduced and referred to the committee on claims, 351. Reported favorably and committed to the committee of the whole, 520. Ordered to a third reading, 808. Bill passed, 871.

Assembly Journal, 1870. Senate bill received and ordered to a third reading, 1479. Bill passed, 1502.

Amount claimed, $6,848.

Award:

Under this act the Canal Appraisers allowed the sum of $1,819.

This bill was not signed by the Governor, jurisdiction being conferred upon Canal Appraisers by general law to determine said claim. (See chapter, 321, Laws of 1870.)

Mrs. Elmira Seymour.

(See E. D. Sherwood and others.)

McNeil Seymour.

(See Amelia C. Vernam.)

Daniel Sharp.

(See George Quinn.)

Peter Shea.

(See Richard Reed and others.)

Jane Shearman.

(See Utica Cotton Company.)

Giles Shell and Others.

Charles Regel, William Krall, Christian Miller, Charles Papke, Michael Wilke, Charles Sahr, William L. Wurl, Frederick Melcher, William Wendt, William Wright, Martin Wilke, Charles Belling, William Fritz, Frederick Gosskoff, Daniel C. Jacobs and John Chadwick.

Nature of Claim:

Compensation for flooding their lands in the town of Wheatfield, Niagara county, by reason of the defective condition of the dyke and ditch on the bank of Tonawanda creek.

Legislative Action:

Senate Journal, 1868. Petition presented and referred to the committee on claims, 134. Reported favorably by bill and committed to the committee of the whole, 337. Ordered to a third reading, 754. Bill passed 756.

Assembly Journal, 1868. Bill received and referred to the committee on claims, with power to report complete, 1334. Ordered to a third reading, 1390. Bill passed, 1529. (See Laws of 1868, chapter 873.)

Award:

Under this act the Canal Appraisers have made the following awards:

	Amount claimed.	Amount allowed.
Giles Shell	$8,691 16	$1,140 00
Charles Regel	482 70	75 00
William Krall	826 00	105 00
Christian Miller	1,748 00	No award.
Charles Papke	419 37	60 00
Michael Wilke	658 88	60 00
Charles Sahr	1,600 34	300 00
William Wurl	2,180 25	100 00
Frederick Melcher	463 14	60 00
William Wendt	612 18	218 00
Alice Wright	1,401 60	120 00
Martin F. Wilke	449 88	60 00
Charles Belling	705 00	240 00
William Fritz	831 42	150 00
Christian Grosskopf	5,711 00	730 00
Daniel C. Jacobs	6,097 73	1,142 50
John Chadwick	1,713 00	No award.

John Sheridan.

(See B. H. Clark and others.)

George B. Sherill.

(See Amariah Holbrook.)

James H. Sherrill.

Nature of Claim:

Extra compensation under contract for constructing a stone dam across the Mohawk river at Cohoes.

Legislative Action:

Senate Journal, 1870. Bill introduced and referred to the committee on claims, 421. Assembly bill received and referred to the committee on claims, 576. Reported favorably and committed to the committee of the whole, 640. Ordered to a third reading, 808. Bill passed, 933.

Assembly Journal, 1870. Bill reported favorably and committed to the committee of the whole, 412. Ordered to a third reading, 827. Bill passed, 860. (See Laws of 1870, chapter 543.)

Under this act no award has yet been made.

E. D. Sherwood and others.

E. D. Larkin, Elijah Thompson, James Patten, James M. Coleman, E. G. Gilson, William Nightingale, Almira Seymour, C. C. Platt, Myron Whiting, William Cole, Martin Green, Zarah Berry, John C. Munro, E. E. Veeder, James Preslow, David A. Munro and S. B. Rowe.

Nature of Claim:

Compensation for damages to their lands, caused by the giving way of the State dam across Nine Mile creek, at the foot of Otisco lake.

Legislative Action:

Senate Journal, 1870. Petition presented and referred to the committee on claims, 42.

James D. Shuler (estate of).

Nature of Claim:

Compensation for lands in the enlargement of the Erie canal at Lockport.

Legislative Action:

Senate Journal, 1868. Petition presented and referred to the committee on claims, 357. Reported favorably by bill and referred to the committee of the whole, 600. Ordered to a third reading, 658. Bill passed, 665.

Assembly Journal, 1868. Bill received and referred to the committee on claims, 1030. Reported favorably and committed to the committee of the whole, 1297. Ordered to a third reading, 1496. Bill passed, 1593. (See Laws of 1868, chapter 759.)

Amount claimed, $5,000.

Award:

Under this act the Canal Appraisers have allowed the sum of $3,350.

John Sinclair.

(See Ovid Plumb and others.)

Skaneateles Outlet.

(See Laws of 1868, chapter 330.)

Under this law the Canal Appraisers are authorized and empowered to hear all claims for damages, by any person or persons, corporation or company, owning or occupying any water power on said outlet, by reason of the obstructing or withholding of its waters by the State or its officers.

[NOTE.—The books of the Appraisers do not designate the names of the claimants under this act. For claims and awards, see supplement.]

Thomas C. Sleeper.

(See Ovid Plumb and others.)

Ezekiel Smith.

(See Erskine G. Clark and others.)

Gerrit Smith and others.

Jonathan D. Ledyard and the legal representatives of Hamilton Murray, deceased.

Nature of Claim:

Compensation for lands taken in the enlargement of the Oswego canal.

Legislative Action:

Senate Journal, 1869. Message from the Assembly requesting the transmission of papers, 51. So ordered.

Senate Journal, 1870. Papers taken from the files and referred to the committee on claims, 48.

Laura P. Smith.

Nature of Claim:

Compensation for damages in loss of land and timber sliding into the Genesee Valley canal, by reason of the defective condition thereof.

Legislative Action:

Senate Journal, 1870. Petition presented and referred to the committee on claims, 376. Bill introduced and referred to the committee on claims, 377. Reported favorably and committed to the committee of the whole, 736. Ordered to a third reading, 809. Bill passed, 869.

Assembly Journal, 1870. Senate bill received and referred to the committee on claims, 1479. Reported favorably and committed to the committee of the whole, 1634. Ordered to a third reading, 1638.

Susan M. Smith, Mary A. Smith, Maria Smith and Joseph Smith.

(See J. J. Burton and others.)

Edmund H. Smith.

Nature of Claim:

To have certain moneys arising from mortgage sale by Loan Commissioners, and paid into Comptroller's office, refunded.

Legislative Action:

Senate Journal, 1868. Petition presented and referred to the committee on finance, 42.

Clark Snook (assignee of Henry S. and Sheldon S. Pratt).

Nature of Claims:

Extra compensation, as contractor for repairs, of superintendent section No. 2 of the Champlain canal, for rebuilding the Wood creek culvert.

Legislative Action:

Senate Journal, 1870. Petition presented and referred to the committee on claims, 143. Bill introduced and referred to the committee on claims, 147. Reported favorably and recommitted to the committee on claims, 520. Reported by a majority of the committee, and committed to the committee of the whole, 530. Ordered to a third reading, 808. Bill passed, 869.

Assembly Journal, 1870. Senate bill received and substituted for Assembly bill, 1478. Ordered to a third reading, 1493. Bill passed, 1765.

This bill was vetoed by the Governor.

Ezekiel Spencer.

Nature of Claim:

Compensation for damages to lands and crops of claimant in the town of German Flats, flooded by the waters of Falmer creek July, 1863.

Legislative Action:

Senate Journal, 1870. Petition presented and referred to the committee on claims, 440. Bill introduced and referred to the same committee, 442. Reported favorably and committed to the committee of the whole, 819.

Henry Storms.

Nature of Claim:

Compensation for services rendered, as Commissary-General of the State of New York.

Legislative Action:

Senate Journal, 1870. Bill introduced and referred to the committee on finance, 819.

Assembly Journal, 1870. Petition presented and referred to the committee on militia, 183.

H. D. H. Snyder, Jr.

(See Linus R. Clark and others.)

Lyman A. Spalding and others.

Nature of Claim:

Compensation for damages sustained by reason of diversion of surplus water of Erie canal at Lockport.

Legislative Action:

Senate Journal, 1866. Petition presented and referred to the committee on canals, 149. Committee discharged. Petition referred to committee on claims. Adverse report. Agreed to, 945. (See Senate document No. 90 of 1866.)

Isaac Sparks.

Nature of Claim:

Compensation for damages to lands of claimant in town of Minden, Montgomery county, by reason of a culvert under Erie canal, the bed of stream above and below said culvert filling up with gravel, causing water to overflow on lands, &c.

Legislative Action:

Senate Journal, 1866. Bill introduced and referred to the committee on claims, 108. Adverse report. Laid on table, 461. (See Senate document No. 65 of 1866.)

George Spies.

(See Linus R. Clark and others.)

James Stack.

(See Erskine G. Clark and others.)

James F. Starbuck.

(See Linus R. Clark and others.)

Josiah A. Stearns.

(See Ovid Plumb and others.)

John A. Sterling.

(See Ovid Plumb and others.)

Hugh Story.

(See Erskine G. Clark and others.)

E. Benedict Strong.

(See Richard Reed and others.)

Lorenzo E. Swan.

Nature of Claim:

Compensation for damages caused by the giving way of the bulkheads or gates made to control the canal reservoir of Cazenovia lake, March 17, 1865, whereby the dam of petitioner was carried away and his water-power rendered useless for ten months.

Legislative Action:

Senate Journal, 1866. Petition presented and referred to the committee on claims, 149. Adverse report, agreed to, 945. (See Senate document No. 96, of 1866.)

Bernardus Swartwout.

(See John Fitzpatrick.)

John M. Swinerton.

(See Richard Reed and others.)

Henry H. Ten Broeck.

Nature of Claim:

Compensation for land taken by the State in constructing a side-cut at Waterford Champlain canal, in 1861.

Legislative Action:

Senate Journal, 1866. Bill introduced and referred to the committee on claims, 94. Reported favorably and referred to the committee of the whole, 442. Ordered to a third reading, 584. Bill passed, 608.

Assembly Journal, 1866. Bill received and referred to the committee on claims, 1121. Reported favorably and referred to the committee of the whole, 1321. Ordered to a third reading, 1660. Bill passed, 1690. (See Senate document No. 59, of 1866.)

Under this act no award has yet been made. (See Laws of 1866, chapter 882.)

Maria Ten Broeck.

Nature of Claim:

The same as in the case of Henry Ten Broeck.

Legislative Action:

Senate Journal, 1866. Bill introduced and referred to the committee on claims, 94. Reported favorably and referred to the committee of the whole, 442. Ordered to a third reading, 584. Passed, 608. (See Senate document No. 58, of 1866.)

Assembly Journal, 1866. Bill received and referred to the committee on claims, 1121. Reported favorably and referred to the committee of the whole, 1321. Ordered to a third reading, 1660. Passed, 1691.

Under this act no award has yet been made. (See **Laws of** 1866, chapter 891.)

Elizabeth Thompson.

Nature of Claim :

Compensation for damages to lands of claimant, caused by the leakage of the enlarged Erie canal, in the town of De Witt, Onondaga county.

Legislative Action :

Senate Journal, 1870. Bill introduced and referred to the committee on claims, 381. Reported favorably and committed to the committee of the whole, 745. Ordered to a third reading, 809. Bill passed, 870.

Assembly Journal, 1870. Senate bill received and substituted for Assembly bill, 1478. Reported favorably and committed to the committee of the whole, 1638.

William T. Thompson.

(See Brackett H. Clark and others.)

Elijah Thompson.

(See E. D. Sherwood and others.)

William Thorn and others.

Nature of Claim:

Relief for damage done by the Erie canal, across Cayuga marshes.

Legislative Action:

Senate Journal, 1868. Petition presented and referred to the committee on canals, 160.

Benjamin F. Thurber.

Nature of Claim:

Compensation for damages to his property in the town of Corning, caused by the break in the embankment forming part of the dam at the head of the Chemung canal, and of the incompletion of the State lock above said dam, at the head of the Chemung canal feeder.

Legislative Action

Senate Journal, 1870. Bill introduced and referred to the committee on claims, 342.

John Tilley.

Nature of Claim:

Compensation for damages to the manufactory of petitioner in West Troy, by reason of the overflow in the side canal, constructed at that place.

Legislative Action:

Senate Journal, 1867. Petition presented and referred to the committee on claims, 77. Reported adversely, in writing. Report agreed to, 585. (See Senate document No. 62, 1867.)

James Toole.

(See Erskine G. Clark and others.)

Job Traffam.

(See Linus R. Clark and others.)

Leander Traffam.

(See Linus R. Clark and others.)

Treman and Banks.

(Ovid Plumb and others.)

Charles N. Tuttle.

(See Edward Mynders and others.)

George A. Underhill.

(See Erskine G. Clark and others.)

Bloomer Underhill.

(See Erskine G. Clark and others.)

Utica Cotton Company and Jane Shearman.

Nature of Claim:

Compensation for damages in the loss of three horses, two barns and other property, swept away by the waters of Sadaquada creek, by reason of the incapacity of the arches of the aqueduct of the Chenango canal, over said creek.

Legislative Action:

Senate Journal, 1870. Petition presented and referred to the committee on claims, 35. Reported favorably by bill and committed to the committee of the whole, 218. Ordered to a third reading, 323 Bill passed 330.

Assembly Journal, 1870. Senate bill received and referred to the committee on claims, 494. Reported favorably and committed to the committee of the whole, 735. Ordered to a third reading, 829. Bill passed 864. (See Laws of 1870, chapter 149.)

No award has yet been made in this case.

Nicholas Van De Bogert and Giles Van De Bogert.

Nature of Claim:

Compensation for flooding their lands, by reason of the defective banks of the Erie canal in the city of Schenectady.

Legislative Action:

Senate Journal, 1869. Bill introduced and referred to the committee on claims, 162. Reported favorably and committed to the committee of the whole, 508. Ordered to a third reading, 926. Bill passed, 951.

Assembly Journal, 1869. Bill introduced and referred to the committee on claims, 918. Senate bill received and referred to the committee on claims, 1814. Reported favorably and committed to the committee of the whole, 1904.

Van Namer and Smith.

(See Linus R. Clark and others.)

Amelia C. Vernam and McNeil Seymour.

Nature of Claim:

Remuneration for two ice breakers and other property, belonging to Abraham Vernam, deceased, taken by R. C. Dorn, Superintendent of section No. 1, Erie canal.

Legislative Action:

Senate Journal, 1866. Petition presented and referred to the committee on claims, 33. Bill received from the Assembly, 813. Referred to the committee on claims. Reported favorably with amendments, and referred to the committee of the whole, 931. Ordered to a third reading, 1005. Passed, 1015.

Assembly Journal, 1866. Petition presented and referred to committee on claims. Reported favorably. Bill introduced and referred to the committee of the whole and ordered to a third reading, 1400. Bill passed, 1432.

Amount claimed, $8,623.99.

Award:

Under this act the Canal Board allowed the sum of $5,714.

E. E. Veeder.

(See E. D. Sherwood and others.)

John Vischer.

Nature of Claim:

Compensation for damages sustained in loss of timber, lumber, saw logs, buildings, shingles and machinery, carried away, injured and destroyed in consequence of a break in the embankment forming a part of the canal dam at the head of the Chemung canal feeder in the town of Corning.

Legislative Action:

Senate Journal, 1870. Bill introduced and referred to the committee on claims, 301. Reported favorably and committed to the committee of the whole, 487. Ordered to a third reading, 766. Bill passed, 867.

Assembly Journal, 1870. Senate bill received and referred to the committee on claims, with power to report complete, 1478. Reported complete and ordered to a third reading, 1521.

Charles Volmer.

(See Linus R. Clark and others.)

Vulcan Iron Works.

Nature of Claim:

Compensation for damages to a locomotive precipitated into the canal at Buffalo, by reason of the defective bridge over the Erie canal on Commercial street in said city.

Legislative Action:

Senate Journal, 1868. Petition presented and referred to the committee on claims, 75. Reported adversely in writing. Report agreed to, 288. (See Senate document No. 60.)

Craig B. Wadsworth.

(See D. H. Fitzhugh.)

Daniel Wagner and Andrew Wagner.

(See Laura A. Poole and others.)

Eben B. Wait and others.

Nature of Claim:

Compensation for damage to their water power and paper-mill, at Little Falls, N. Y., by the Rocky Rift dam and the placing of flush boards thereon.

Legislative Action:

Senate Journal, 1866. Petition presented and referred to the committee on claims, 254.

Theodocia Wall and others.

Amasa P. Hart (Oliver Breed, Glass, Breed & Co., Joseph J. Glass, Edwin P. Hopkins), George G. Breed, Edmund Murray and Daniel Hubbard, claimed ——

Nature of Claim:

Compensation for damages to lands, buildings and mill property of claimants, in consequence of rebuilding the dam on the Oswego river at Phenix.

Legislative Action:

Senate Journal, 1868. Bill introduced and referred to the committee on claims, 106. Reported favorably and committed to the committee of the whole, 211. Ordered to a third reading, 281. Bill lost, 294. Reconsidered and passed, 299.

Assembly Journal, 1868. Bill received and referred to the committee on claims, 554. Reported favorably and committed to the committee of the whole, 695. Ordered to a third reading, 849. Bill passed, 1016.

Under this act the Canal Appraisers have made the following awards:

	Amount claimed.	Amount allowed
Joseph J. Glass, Oliver Breed, Edwin P. Hopkins (firm Glass, Breed & Co)	$21,000 00	$14,250 00
Daniel Hubbard	3,290 00	1,140 00
Amasa P. Hart	21,250 00	10,431 00
Theodocia Wall	27,300 00	7,362 40
Edmund Merry and George G. Breed	26,810 00	12,363 30

J. B. Warren.

(See J. J. Burton and others.)

Watertown Lock Works.

(See Linus R. Clark and others.)

Watertown Paper Company.

(See Linus R. Clark and others.)

Charles Weatherby.

(See Linus R. Clark and others.)

Hiram Weeks.

Nature of Claim:

Compensation for damages to his property in the town of Corning, March, 1865, by reason of a defect in the embankment of the Chemung river, in connection with the Chemung canal.

Legislative Action:

Senate Journal, 1869. Bill introduced and referred to the committee on claims, 46. Reported favorably and committed to the committee of the whole, 80. Ordered to a third reading, 106. Bill passed, 111.

Assembly Journal, 1869. Bill received and referred to the committee on claims, 182. Reported favorably, 240. Ordered to a third reading, 376. Bill passed, 413. (See Laws of 1869, chapter 36.)

Amount clamed, $2,730.00.

Award:

Under this act the Canal Appraisers allowed the sum of $2,891.52.

Charles Weiss.

Nature of Claim:

Compensation for injuries to his person, caused by being shot while doing patrol duty.

Legislative Action:

Senate Journal, 1868. Message received from the Assembly requesting the transmission of papers, 212.

[NOTE.—In 1869, a bill was introduced in the Assembly for the payment of the claim, and became a law.] (See Laws of 1869, chapter 562.)

William Wendt.

(See Giles Shell and others.)

West and Taggert.

(See Linus R. Clark and others.)

John E. Westlake and others.

Nature of Claim:

Compensation for damages occasioned to their land by leakage from the Chemung canal feeder.

Legislative Action:

Senate Journal, 1867. Petition presented and referred to the committee on claims, 55. Reported favorably by bill and committed to the committee of the whole, 767.

Senate Journal, 1868. Papers taken from the files and referred to the committee on claims, 187. Message received from the Assembly requesting transmission of papers. Committee discharged from further consideration, and papers sent to the Assembly, 252.

Senate Journal, 1869. Papers taken from the files and referred to the committee on claims, 268.

Judah Whitcomb.

(See Ovid Plumb and others.)

Myron Whiting.

(See E. D. Sherwood and others.)

Lucy E. Whitney.

(See J. J. Burton and others.)

Robert Wiggins.

(See Erskine G. Clark and others.)

Mary H. Wilcox.

(See B. H. Clark and others.)

Martin Wilke.

(See Giles Shell and others.)

Michael Wilke.

(See Giles Shell and others.)

Samuel D. Willard.

Nature of Claim:

Compensation for lands taken in the enlargement of the Erie canal, and destruction of one-quarter of a mile of post and board fence. Also for ground rent for the lock house since the year 1856.

Legislative Action:

Senate Journal, 1870. Petition presented and referred to the committee on claims, 297. Bill introduced and referred to the same committee, 300. Reported favorably and committed to the committee of the whole, 312. Ordered to a third reading, 439. Bill passed. 448.

Assembly Journal, 1870. Senate bill received and referred to the committee on claims, 661. Reported favorably and committed to the committee of the whole, 979. Ordered to a third reading, 1494.

Stephen Williams.

(See Ovid Plumb and others.)

Charles P. Williams.

See Linus R. Clark and others.)

William Wilson.

(See Linus R. Clark and others.)

Samuel Wood.

(See Erskine G. Clark and others.)

M. C. Woodruff and others.

Nature of Claims:

Papers not found on file, and nature of claim unknown.

Legislative Action:

Senate Journal, 1866. Petition presented and referred to the committee on claims, 161.

John G. Wormley.

(See Lucien Billinghurst and others.)

William Wright.

(See Giles Shell and others.)

Charles T. Wright.

(See John C. Blaisdell and others.)

William L. Wurl.

(See Giles Shell and others.)

Lorenzo Yates.

Nature of Claim:

Compensation for damages in diverting water from his mills to the Genesee Valley canal.

Legislative Action:

Senate Journal, 1867. Petition presented and referred to the committee on claims, 70. Assembly bill received and referred to the committee on claims, 267. Reported adversely and report agreed to, 1119. Bill rejected.

George R. Yaw.

Nature of Claim:

Compensation for damages to his property, caused by dredging out the canal at Buffalo.

Legislative Action:

Senate Journal, 1870. Petition presented and referred to the committee on claims, 37. Reported favorably by bill and committed to the committee of the whole, 469. Ordered to a third reading, 766. Bill passed, 866.

Assembly Journal, 1870. Senate bill received and referred to the committee on claims, to report complete, 1478. Reported complete and ordered to a third reading, 1521.

SUPPLEMENT

SHOWING ALL AWARDS MADE BY THE CANAL BOARD AND CANAL APPRAISERS FROM SEPTEMBER 30TH, 1865, TO SEPTEMBER 30TH, 1870, INCLUSIVE; TOGETHER WITH ALL CLAIMS PRESENTED TO THE CANAL BOARD AND CANAL APPRAISERS FOR THE SAME PERIOD.

Claims before the Canal Board are marked by an asterisk.

STATEMENT OF AWARDS.

	Amount claimed.	Amount allowed.
Ackerman, Herman	$4,000 00	$3,870 46
Ackels, John	3,361 90	1,070 00
Adams & Close	25,000 00	12,540 00
Adams & Close	25,000 00	5,885 00
Addle, Joseph	500 00	417 30
Adams, Harry H	1,246 00	403 56
Allen & Burchard	1,177 57	93 78
Albany Pier Company	9,500 00	Nothing
Albany Pier Company	10,663 75	10,633 75
Allen, William T	100 00	110 50
Allen, Nancy G	200 00	160 50
Aldrich, Benedict, (deceased,) estate of	1,085 66	413 60
Ames, George*	Not stated	4,429 00
Ames, S. C*	Not stated	4,297 05
Angus, Charlotte	652 00	652 00
Arthur, Alfred	900 00	620 00
Armstrong, Enoch B	1,015 00	1,169 13
Arnold, Justin*	Not stated	3,992 62
Austin, De Witt F	6,500 00	2,140 00
Avery, William*	Not stated	23,000 00
Avery, William, & Company*	Not stated	150 00
Ayer, Warren	2,995 00	1,166 30
Bassett, Norton & Bassett, (assignees of Bassett & Mills)	5,517 00	2,240 75

	Amount claimed.	Amount allowed.
Barry, Catherine	$100 00	$100 00
Barrow, Roger	750 00	600 00
Bassett, Norton	1,000 00	837 37
Baker, Lewis A	1,200 00	610 00
Barry, David	700 00	262 00
Barse, James	1,000 00	637 50
Bailey, Silas	2,000 00	2,000 00
Barnes & Coleman	3,546 00	489 52
Barnes, William & J. W	460 00	97 24
Bannister & Weeks	3,450 62	2,762 50
Barber, Joel	1,500 00	1,266 29
Barber, Wyllis*	Not stated	90 00
Baer, John	2,273 50	1,672 00
Barse, James	275 00	323 13
Babcock, William A	50 00	53 50
Ball, Elizabeth, and others	595 00	546 97
Balch, Elnora and Maria	296 00	259 00
Bartholomew, Henry M	2,730 00	868 68
Banks, Alonzo	5,163 40	5,170 40
Benedict, Ebenezer	200 00	60 00
Berrus, Sherman & Calvin	1,000 00	Nothing
Benjamin, Le Grand	10,000 00	4,500 00
Beyer, Philip, Jacob and George	3,000 00	255 00
Betts, Ira	2,450 00	1,677 00
Belling, Charles	705 00	240 00
Benjamin, Delos	460 00	335 00
Bennett, Roswell G	3,286 00	2,777 00
Beach, Nelson J	5,600 00	100 00
Belden, A. C	2,000 00	2,140 00
Becker, Martin	1,000 00	1,186 57
Betts, Cordelia E., (estate of)	4,000 00	3,840 00
Beary, William	4,500 00	Nothing
Behen, J. F.*	Not stated	100 00
Belden, James J*	Not stated	8,265 86
Bellows, James*	Not stated	22,500 00
Benjamin, Allen	1,704 00	1,117 20
Bibbins, Samuel	1,148 00	934 32

	Amount claimed.	Amount allowed.
Bissell, Andrew H.	$1,218 00	$1,431 15
Bishop, John	600 00	217 75
Billinghurst, Lucien	276 00	367 77
Bissell, Charlotte (executrix)	3,548 70	3,795 72
Bloodgood, Mary	25,000 00	875 54
Blaisdell, John C.	230 00	278 30
Blodgett, Andrew	451 00	226 53
Bloodgood, Winfield	3,695 00	2,026 47
Bowman, Jacob L.	1,200 00	1,147 50
Boardman, Olcott P.	1,000 00	102 00
Boughton, Peter	1,000 00	1,186 57
Bolt, Douglass & French	Not stated	6,800 00
Bordwell, William	314 95	267 50
Botsford, Augustus	2,176 26	2,066 55
Brown, Wellington	2,300 00	1,685 00
Brown, Caleb	750 00	400 00
Breiner, Frederick	800 00	500 00
Brooks, James H.	1,000 00	744 80
Brigham, Louisa (administratrix)	1,200 00	765 00
Brigham, Sullivan	1,100 00	1,100 00
Brown, Samuel	400 00	217 50
Brayell & Hunt,* assignees of Lewis M. Loss *	Not stated	455 50
Brayell, McCann & Dolphin*	Not stated	3,156 75
Breed, Joseph*	Not stated	700 00
Bristol, Fayette (Sec. 3 Genesee Valley canal)*	Not stated	1,913 11
Bristol, Fayette (Sec. 4 Genesee Valley canal)*	Not stated	2,020 10
Brown, Levi H.	Not stated	1,000 00
Brown, Isaac F.	1,662 00	587 50
Briggs, Noah	2,146 50	1,148 14
Brown, Geo.	1,368 00	552 25
Bronson Eli A.	756 00	978 78
Burdick, Charles	1,000 00	250 00
Burdick, James	500 00	150 00
Burdick, Stephen	500 00	320 00

	Amount claimed.	Amount allowed.
Burdick, Calvin	$2,600 00	$600 00
Burdick, Nathan	2,000 00	660 00
Bull, Henry	13,600 00	3,524 06
Budd, Charles D	250 00	90 00
Burt, Ira	400 00	300 00
Buckingham, Mary	100 00	96 00
Butler, William	1,500 00	1,020 00
Buck, Edwin	735 00	106 50
Butterfield, Oliver	330 00	399 30
Burdick, Mathew T	6,150 00	1,845 00
Burger, John	2,000 00	285 00
Buckley, Patrick	973 00	483 07
Burnett, A. J.	500 00	267 50
Burnett, William H	300 00	214 00
Burdick, S. E.	460 00	540 50
Burdick, Henry	780 00	799 00
Rurroughs, Silas	369 20	267 50
Burton, Benjamin	4,135 00	1,835 40
Buckley, Patrick	407 50	400 00
Byrne, Michael	150 00	181 50
Carter, Hiram	220 00	130 00
Carter, George	180 00	130 98
Campbell, Conley E	1,860 00	713 64
Cayuga & Seneca Bridge Co	3,000 00	250 00
Casey, Patrick	250 00	Nothing
Case, William H.	550 00	Nothing
Card, Daniel	1,100 00	312 00
Casler, Alfred (estate of)	1,270 00	218 40
Carney, James	500 00	282 20
Casler, Richard M	500 00	413 50
Casler, Henry	375 00	262 50
Cagger, Peter	8,000 00	7,806 80
Casler Alfred (estate of)	1,270 00	228 20
Cayuga & Seneca Bridge Co	3,000 00	1,500 00
Carrington, Frederick T	108,500 00	36,349 00
Campbell, John G. (estate of)	6,000 00	3,178 00
Cary, Rody	115 00	115 00
Cary, Rody	235 50	116 93

	Amount claimed.	Amount allowed.
Cady, H. T.*	Not stated	$311 70
Caldwell, James*	Not stated	450 00
Case, Charles E*	Not stated	......
Case, George M. (assignee of George Collins)	Not stated	8,342 44
Canada Minerva	$200 00	193 88
Casterton, Thomas	1,700 00	1,997 50
Camp, James F	5,070 00	2,954 70
Camp, Roswell, 2d	1,295 00	714 09
Carnochan, Mary	1,478 00	701 47
Catlin, Nathaniel	2,710 00	922 26
Campbell, Conley E	2,106 27	2,162 16
Childs, Philander	1,350 00	356 40
Chaphy, Lucy	500 00	500 00
Chamberlain, J. P. (assignee, &c)	3,644 43	3,195 00
Champlin, Marshall B	360 00	340 00
Chadwick, Holland W., Jr	1,500 00	276 25
Chaffee, Norman J	3,000 00	3,597 78
Cheever, Samuel	2,000 00	1,152 00
Churchill, Peter	3,693 50	2,371 23
Churchill, Ward	1,134 10	910 12
Churchill, William	12,208 80	10,379 00
Champlin, Jabez	1,000 00	605 00
Champlin, Jabez	1,585 00	1,099 30
Cleveland, Uriah A. (executor)	2,800 00	1,005 00
Closson, Amanda	700 00	150 00
Clark, Maria	2,000 00	1,733 50
Clapper, Enoch	100 00	Nothing
Clapper, Enoch	100 00	100 00
Close & Adams	10,322 00	3,420 00
Clapp, James H	737 00	735 09
Clark, Peter W.*	Not stated	613 17
Clark, George	349 80	280 71
Cleveland, Jerome	662 50	748 48
Cleveland, Paschal H	425 00	499 38
Clifford, Richard	3,480 00	1,011 67
Constable, James	2,822 00	1,235 00
Cookingham, Peter	1,500 00	465 00

	Amount claimed.	Amount allowed.
Copeland, John	$4,600 00	$1,680 00
Coyle, Patrick H	500 00	101 40
Cole, Madison A. & Elizabeth	300 00	130 50
Com'rs Highways, Portville	3,000 00	Nothing
Coapman, Lydia H	200 00	150 00
Coe, Curtis	250 00	115 00
Cook, Sarah M	600 00	300 00
Cole, Samuel J	4,025 00	935 00
Cooney, Nicholas	8,000 00	6,982 85
Cooney, Patrick	3,000 00	2,154 14
Conroy, Charles	4,500 00	Nothing.
Cook, Joseph J	2,500 00	1,988 05
Cook, Andrew	3,300 00	2,893 40
Costello, Thomas (widow and heirs of)	500 00	265 50
Coleman, Obadiah	675 00	221 00
Corneau & Soule	2,500 00	1,206 61
Coburn, Andrew & Ebenezer	2,550 00	893 45
Coon, Alanson, G.*	Not stated	816 80
Cooley, Rosannah	360 11	423 00
Compson, Stephen	300 00	300 00
Covell, George W	1,945 00	2,197 25
Covell, Stephen A	520 00	473 91
Cogswell, George F	762 66	385 20
Cooper, George & Samuel	4,080 00	2,368 00
Coe, Samuel N	1,610 00	1,345 31
Coston, Charles C	1,318 36	1,307 46
Crandall, Joseph	1,200 00	1,091 55
Crandall, Roswell A	500 00	490 20
Crandle, Richard S	500 00	Nothing.
Crandle, Seth	350 00	Nothing.
Craig, John & Stewart	820 00	640 87
Cramer, George W	985 00	741 50
Crain, Almiron W. & Perry P	5,000 00	4,000 00
Crawford, Joseph	900 00	Not allo'd.
Crossman & Force	3,000 00	267 50
Crysler, Martin	2,000 00	912 00
Crane, George	225 00	192 60

	Amount claimed.	Amount allowed.
Cushing, F. A. & A. A.	$1,500 00	$1,791 23
Davis, Jonathan	4,250 00	1,682 97
Davis, Richard B.	2,500 00	2,000 00
Dayan, A. G. & Jane H. L.	1,900 00	600 00
Dalton, James	300 00	Nothing.
Daly, Terance	390 00	471 90
Damon, Clark	350 00	318 70
Danolds, Charles A.*	Not stated	10,832 40
Davis, Charles*	Not stated	333 12
Davis, John A	2,034 75	1,282 00
Daniels, Amos	4,185 00	1,792 08
Davis, Alonzo	1,500 00	1,500 00
Davis, Alonzo	2,000 00	1,936 00
Davison, Josiah L.	2,062 00	820 15
Devereaux, Albert	400 00	300 00
De Kay, Abiah F.	2,500 00	Nothing
De Kay, Abiah F. (reheard)	2,500 00	312 00
De Mont, George	500 00	40 00
De Grand, Benjamin	10,000 00	3,500 00
De Mont, William	1,000 00	450 00
Devendorf, Cornelius V.	210 00	117 50
Devendorf, Cornelius V. (reheard)	210 00	Nothing
Dewey, Edwin W.	500 00	429 42
Dewey, George W.	500 00	330 33
Devereaux, Patrick	2,000 00	1,701 00
Denio, Salina	2,230 00	1,446 00
De Kay, Abiah F.	2,500 00	Nothing
De Graw, Charles J.*	Not stated	21,530 37
De Graw, Charles J.*	Not stated	24,000 00
De Groat, Lorenzo N.	1,100 00	813 15
Dean, William	1,274 20	1,278 75
Devereaux, Patrick	810 00	530 41
Dixon & White	4,000 00	866 66
Dixon, James	2,150 00	1,504 50
Dickerson & Kennedy	15,686 12	4,588 12
Dinsmore, George*	Not stated	7,493 49
Dibble, Leroy A.	55 85	59 76

	Amount claimed.	Amount allowed.
Douglas, Nathan W	$1,000 00	$200 00
Dominick, Francis J	300 00	120 00
Donaldson, Samuel*	Not stated	18,636 93
Driggs, Sterling	910 00	323 00
Drummond, William	180 00	193 88
Dumpsey, Michael	200 00	50 00
Dygert, Jonathan	400 00	360 59
Dyer, Burton H	1,000 00	963 00
Egan, Charles	95 00	Nothing
Egan, Charles	95 00	75 00
Earlls & Tallman	1,457 22	602 22
Earlls, Andrew J	532 00	303 88
Earll, George H. & Co	835 00	546 98
Earlls, Thayer & Co	14,473 31	6,295 18
Earl, Samuel*	Not stated	1,000 00
Eastman, J. Russell (agent for Lucy Eastman)	237 20	200 41
Edwards, Hiram K	975 00	955 80
Edgar, William H	679 02	439 12
Edgarton, Ralph H	2,000 00	700 00
Edwards, John	377 40	352 40
Eddy, Sarah A	512 00	356 70
Eggleston, John	2,500 00	1,890 38
Ellis, Charles A	1,000 00	800 00
Eldridge, Goyen R. & Lewis	3,652 00	1,443 43
Eldridge, Margaret	2,569 00	974 70
Ely, Ann S	7,500 00	2,852 62
Emmons, John W	1,000 00	850 00
Emmons, Harriet M	150 00	255 00
Emmons, Edward N	200 00	170 00
Emmons, Samuel	300 00	255 00
Enders, Peter J	800 00	570 00
Evans, Evan & James	450 00	668 00
Evans, William	2,585 92	1,964 92
Evarts & Evans	1,806 00	1,356 10
Farwell, Abram M	1,500 00	883 40
Fancher, Ira, Jr	2,000 00	2,341 00

	Amount claimed.	Amount allowed.
Fayle, Thomas	$2,500 00	$3,018 85
Fisher, Bradley	1,000 00	400 00
Filkins, Barnet	1,800 00	1,204 16
Fitzpatrick, John*	Not stated	7,629 77
Fitzgerald & Kane	300 00	321 00
Fletcher, Wentworth & Co	4,380 00	1,380 00
Foster, Alban	3,500 00	600 00
Fox, Oliva	1,625 00	1,218 88
Frazier, Barbara M	320 00	Nothing
Frazier, Barbara M. (reheard)	320 00	141 00
French, Albert G	4,536 00	3,078 00
Fritz, William	831 42	150 00
Freeman, Pattison	2,000 00	1,881 00
Fuller, James B	275 00	75 00
Fuller, David H	4,908 50	4,650 00
Fuller & Manning	6,000 00	Nothing
Gates, Archibald H	9,703 45	1,909 39
Gaston, Schuyler M	1,200 00	940 00
Gaston, Ira	4,000 00	2,980 00
Galligher, James	23,025 00	9,000 00
Gay, Tyler & Hall	6,000 00	3,487 35
Gale, Thomas*	Not stated	904 08
Gale, Thomas (assignee of C. J. DeGraw)*	Not stated	25,997 73
Gale, Thomas*	Not stated	27,297 20
Gale, Thomas	2,475 00	1,875 61
Gale, Thomas & Co	1,500 00	1,189 40
Gardiner, Egbert	100 00	Nothing
Gere, Isaac W	24,700 00	10,500 00
Gear, H. S.*	Not stated.	651 36
Gilmartin, James and Winneford	1,600 00	1,671 00
Gifford, Cordelia C	2,500 00	1,106 60
Gifford, Cordelia	1,044 00	1,198 50
Gillespie, Wyatt C	1,455 92	370 16
Gilchrist, James H	1,457 00	1,200 00
Glasgow, Ralph	500 00	150 00
Glasgow, William	900 00	877 50
Gleason, Sanford J	1,750 00	1,573 35

	Amount claimed.	Amount allowed
Glass, Breed & Co	$21,000 00	$14,250 00
Glann, George and James H	3,731 00	1,536 52
Glancy & Sullivan	600 00	354 00
Glann, William	5,655 00	1,741 29
Goff, William	1,879 29	1,673 00
Gould, Samuel A	1,000 00	Nothing
Gould, Samuel A	2,500 00	1,284 00
Gould, George	2,000 00	Nothing
Gould, George H	225 00	226 20
Goodwin, Samuel	800 00	280 00
Goodwin, Samuel	800 00	644 50
Goit, James H. & Co	525 00	525 00
Godspeed, Joel J	11,300 00	3,718 25
Goodrich, Edwin	2,543 00	1,340 71
Graves, Thomas J	400 00	60 00
Graves, Nathan	250 00	Nothing
Graves, Nathan	225 00	200 00
Graves, Thomas J	400 00	200 00
Greaser, William	200 00	170 00
Greenleaf, Susan	400 00	72 60
Greeno, Oliver	250 00	200 00
Greeno, Laton M	475 00	245 00
Green, D. M.*	Not stated	563 72
Green, Job, Jr	14,385 00	6,805 50
Grattan, Patrick	7,040 00	100 00
Griffin, Erastus W	100 00	42 80
Griffin, Orrin	3,699 05	2,637 23
Grosskopf, Christiane	5,711 00	730 00
Grinnell, Seymour	390 00	321 00
Groesbeck, Cornelius	2,940 00	1,140 23
Groesbeck, Isaac W	1,220 00	541 26
Groesbeck, Isaac W	1,960 00	996 92
Grosskopft, Henry	300 00	115 00
Guerin, Daniel	220 00	266 20
Gutchess, Margaret E	1,000 00	500 00
Haggerty, John	2,372 91	1,288 40
Harman & Cocks	1,622 22	1,616 87

	Amount claimed.	Amount allowed.
Halsey, Luther H.	$500 00	$500 00
Hagar & Yorkey	3,000 00	2,832 00
Haskins, James P.	Not stated	6,449 00
Hart, Amasa P.	21,250 00	10,431 00
Harter, Peter	100 00	Nothing
Harter, Peter (reheard)	100 00	100 00
Hatch, Janus H.	475 00	284 00
Hayden, Julia	825 00	456 00
Harnden, Laura	600 00	428 00
Hathaway, John M.	400 00	396 00
Hayden, Ezra and others	18,040 00	13,680 00
Hardy, Marvin W.	505 00	165 75
Hall, Mary E.	800 00	290 00
Hall, Entrome	4,000 00	4,372 55
Hannay, Alexander	200 00	Nothing
Harmon, Eleazor and others	1,000 00	850 00
Hammond & Johnson*	Not stated	23,695 13
Hale, Francis H.	2,258 00	906 02
Haskins, Linus S.	1,790 00	2,103 25
Hagadorn, Sylvanus	259 00	214 00
Harrington, Richard D.	4,850 00	1,826 28
Harris, Henry	1,561 00	832 46
Harvey, John	8,078 50	10,518 70
Hardy, Lyman B.	4,000 00	2,132 50
Hess, Frederick	105 00	44 00
Helmer, David	600 00	Nothing
Helmer, David (reheard)	600 00	50 00
Heath, Henry	300 00	Not allo'd
Heckle, Michael	350 00	345 68
Hennessey, Mary	890 00	704 06
Heath, Geo.*	Not stated	7,500 00
Higby, Harlow,	600 00	300 00
Hitchcock, Albert	292 00	Nothing
Hitchcock, Albert (reheard)	292 00	117 50
Higginbotham, Sands	750 00	642 00
Hill, Hiram	1,150 00	398 44
Hinman, Mary	3,260 58	790 94

	Amount claimed.	Amount allowed.
Hill, Timothy	$1,925 01	$1,393 81
Hillyer, Myron	3,419 15	2,613 21
Hinman, Mary	345 00	262 50
Hopkins, John W. and Nancy	400 00	230 00
Howard, Dean S. and Anna A. L	1,010 00	175 00
Howard, D. S	2,200 00	225 00
Horton, Michael	800 00	600 00
Hoadly, Lyman	200 00	93 50
Howell, Lewis B	8,000 00	Nothing
Howell, Lewis B	12,000 00	5,985 75
Horan, Patrick	3,375 00	1,700 00
Horton, Wilson and John B	300 00	300 00
Hoyt, Jane	1,000 00	994 00
Howland, Phebe Jane	7,800 00	6,093 00
Howland, Robert B	10,100 00	8,080 00
Horan, Patrick .(rehearing)	3,375 00	1,263 50
Hoyt, Ezekial B	1,509 00	831 51
Hopper, James H	500 00	133 10
Hopper, Norman	400 00	36 30
Holmes, Shoemaker and Daniels	15,000 00	5,552 00
Holmes, Shoemaker and Sweet	10,810 00	6,301 20
Holbrook, Lyman*	Not stated	105 00
Holbrook & Sherrill*	Not stated	7,533 83
Hosch, John F., att'y for Philip H. Hosch*	Not stated	5,883 51
Hoessli, Jacob R	7,860 00	3,805 99
Hornless, Albert	65 00	76 38
Houck, George	150 00	173 31
Holmes, John	3,490 00	2,687 35
Hoffman, Gottleib	552 00	562 50
Howell, Edwin W	1,367 12	1,393 62
Hughson, Lorenzo D	3,048 30	1,138 40
Hubbard, Mary B	1,000 00	999 00
Hubbard, Wm. O	5,000 00	4,912 56
Hubbard & North	1,675 00	Nothing
Hunter, Thomas T	7,817 50	Nothing
Hunter, Thomas T. (reheard)	7,817 50	4,652 45
Hunt, Jane	400 00	270 00

	Amount claimed.	Amount allowed.
Hughson, John	$1,002 00	$780 00
Hubbard, Daniel	602 52	276 75
Hunsicker, Elias	1,500 00	1,105 00
Huntley, Henry	700 00	147 20
Ide, Henry, Jr	675 00	601 88
Ingalls, George S	320 00	387 20
Ingerson, David	2,000 00	1,158 70
Jackson, John	2,000 00	689 49
Jacobs, Daniel C	6,097 73	1,142 50
Jameson, Harriet P. and Sarah	Not stated	195 96
James, Henry (by agent)	1,500 00	374 50
Johnson, Horace	150 00	102 00
Johnson, Daniel and Rebecca	8,318 50	5,240 00
Johnson & Gilbert	675 00	389 50
Johnson, Timothy	1,582 25	900 00
Johnson, Sarah E	175 00	100 00
Johnson, Henry S	1,000 00	670 00
Joslin, Hosea F	180 00	211 50
Johnson, Jefferson	810 00	1,079 32
Kelly, Charles R	402 50	305 50
Ketchum, Leander S	900 00	100 00
Ketchum, L. S. (trustees of, &c.)	2,000 00	Nothing
Kelley, Patrick	400 00	342 50
Kendrick, Maria	25,000 00	7,817 00
Kelley, Bridget	200 00	187 25
Kent, Isaac	1,000 00	510 00
Kent, Isaac	304 00	351 33
Kelley, Isaac	759 92	616 87
Kirby, William P	683 00	Nothing
Kirby, William P	683 00	117 50
Kinney, Phineas and Elizabeth (exe'rs, &c.)	1,800 00	1,560 00
Kincade, Alexander	980 00	1,185 80
Kinney, Warren	716 40	601 07
Kimble, Jacob	4,190 00	2,926 00
Kingsbury, John (heirs of)	3,781 20	3,609 37
Knapp, Erastus	400 00	373 10
Kohler, Charles	500 00	Nothing

	Amount claimed.	Amount allowed.
Kohler, David and Charles	$2,849 24	$946 00
Koler, David	500 00	Nothing
Krall, William	826 00	105 00
Larraway & Eaker	6,000 00	267 50
Larraway & Eaker	6,000 00	2,850 00
Lappens, Henry	700 00	736 00
Lamont, Samuel	5,160 00	1,967 73
Lace, John C	2,500 00	521 00
Lamb, Chauncey B	250 00	125 00
Larferleer, H. M. and H. W	1,000 00	Nothing
Larabee, Hamilton S. and Alvin	1,000 00	800 00
Lay, Hiram	1,500 00	350 00
Larraway, Catherine M	250 00	125 00
Larkin, Timothy	1,500 00	400 00
Lamb, William E	160 00	120 00
Lay, Darrow	600 00	Nothing
Lay, Peter and Smith	450 00	400 00
Lawton, Daniel C	1,000 00	380 00
Lane, Chauncey	5,000 00	5,000 00
Lanther, John	675 00	793 13
La Grange, Moses	1,980 00	1,189 59
La Mont, David M	2,712 00	1,184 33
La Mont, Fred S	2,244 00	1,095 10
Layton & Stanbro	841 00	693 00
Layton, Jacob B	685 00	270 00
Leek, Jarvis S	800 00	500 00
Lee & Turner	3,825 00	2,464 21
Lewis, Hiram	1,115 00	756 96
Leennun, Patrick H.*	Not stated	5,571 01
Like, Peter H	640 00	479 16
Leib, Barbara (widow, &c.)	11,000 00	200 00
Linihan, Daniel and wife	300 00	270 00
Little, John H	12,000 00	5,700 00
Loomis, George S	200 00	200 00
Loomis & Griswold	1,000 00	812 45
Long & Smith, executors	3,271 50	425 00
Loniss, Caroline A	300 00	250 00

	Amount claimed.	Amount allowed.
Lord, Henry	$600 00	$255 00
Loniss, Caroline A	350 00	250 00
Lonis, Catherine	275 00	160 00
Loniss, Catharine	260 00	160 00
Loomis, William W	420 00	493 50
Locke, James S	10,488 00	9,562 50
Lord, Jarvis, assignee of James Bellows*	Not stated	30,000 00
Lord, F. N., assignee of J. R. Whitlock*	Not stated	20,812 64
Loss, Lewis M., att'y for Wm. Mudgett*	Not stated	20,285 00
Lyon, Henrietta D	800 00	175 00
Lyon, Lyman R	1,300 00	740 00
Lynch, Rose	100 00	75 00
Martin, Frederick S	20,000 00	15,187 50
Mattison, Nathaniel B	850 00	700 00
Mahar, Lawrence	175 00	75 00
Martin, Philip	800 00	612 00
Mason, Andrew W	2,000 00	1,800 30
Marsh, William	10,000 00	3,869 98
Martin, Russell*	Not stated	9,500 00
Martin, Russell*	Not stated	7,469 54
McClary & Powis	7,000 00	1,141 00
McCleary & Powis	7,000 00	4,646 00
McBride, Michael	500 00	350 00
McGuire, Catharine and others (heirs of)	1,000 00	Nothing
McGrath, John	1,000 00	175 00
McKinley, Jesse	8,000 00	6,112 50
McCann, John	3,000 00	2,194 61
McCrea, Wesson B	2,500 00	2,801 25
McKee, Amanda	350 00	Nothing
McCormick, Anna	250 00	Nothing
McAllister, James	575 00	265 50
McKinley, F. and R	3,500 00	4,210 07
McMahon, William	2,000 00	1,210 09
McCann, Philip	1,800 50	535 00
McCauleff, John (estate of)	659 10	528 93
McIntosh, Ann*	Not stated	500 00
McRay, William*	Not stated	3,087 75

	Amount claimed.	Amount allowed.
Mead, Jeremiah	$250 00	$250 00
Mead, Samuel	2,200 00	1,416 00
Merritt, Isaac (executor, &c.)	10,000 00	7,585 00
Merritt, Isaac (executor, &c.)	7,198 00	1,230 00
Melcher, Frederick	463 14	60 00
Merritt, Isaac (executor, &c.)	7,198 00	6,042 00
Merrick, Andrew J	3,300 00	552 50
Mersereau, George J	2,390 00	770 40
Mersereau, John F. and Grant	5,115 00	1,821 64
Merry & Breed	26,810 00	12,363 30
Mersereau, George J	2,390 00	770 40
Meeker, Elliott	1,012 00	843 75
Minier, John	6,525 50	1,916 00
Minier, Samuel	4,602 75	2,139 00
Middaugh, William	6,000 00	2,850 00
Miller, Ezra	485 60	432 00
Middaugh, Rachel	300 00	300 00
Miles, Sweeting	6,781 25	1,657 50
Milk, Charles G	3,000 00	1,066 00
Millis, Mary Ann	3,350 00	3,825 00
Mills, Myron H.*	Not stated	24,423 09
Mills, Myron H.*	Not stated	7,602 74
Mills, Frederick M.*	Not stated	18,839 65
Mills, Edward A.*	Not stated	1,607 56
Morgan, Samuel	6,060 00	2,350 58
Morgan, Louisa S	100 00	96 00
Morgan, Margaret	150 00	Nothing
Morgan, Margaret (reheard)	150 00	150 00
Montgomery, H., and others, executors, &c.	4,000 00	615 25
Morris, Hannah M. and Harriet	100 00	Nothing
Morton, Thomas	8,603 00	1,564 68
Moreland, Parley	138 00	132 60
Monroe, Daniel C. and John	415 00	221 00
Monroe, James	438 20	442 00
Mogg, Aaron	3,000 00	3,531 95
Morrell, Asa	122 00	136 30
Morse, Harlow	450 00	446 50

	Amount claimed.	Amount allowed.
Morse, Amos	$2,200 00	$805 98
Morgan, Conley M	11,115 00	5,415 83
Morgan, Carter H	8,880 00	3,668 24
Montieth, William*	Not stated	2,047 96
Morey, Michael*	Not stated	1,952 26
Munday, Nicholas S	3,265 00	1,777 50
Murdock, Austin	1,740 00	744 95
Myers, John	560 00	513 06
National Bank of Auburn	27,500 00	22,800 00
Newell & Sperry	4,310 00	635 37
Newville, Alexander	7,540 40	4,892 19
Nichols, Alexander H	1,200 00	200 00
Ninde, Sophronia F	350 00	353 00
Nichols, George	9,668 00	2,972 46
Nichols, John H	280 00	272 05
Niles, James L	3,781 98	1,686 14
Nichols, Charles	2,722 50	1,731 66
Nichols, Justus	3,280 00	2,453 40
Nichols, William	1,780 00	478 80
Norton, Winthrop	560 00	400 00
Norton, Catharine	1,400 00	177 00
O'Brien, James	2,775 00	750 00
O'Brien, Timothy	440 00	96 20
O'Brien, James	1,061 00	700 00
Odell, Samuel W.*	Not stated	2,350 00
O'Connor, Thomas	3,300 00	780 00
Olmstead & Fish	650 00	695 50
Olmstead, Augustus	3,400 00	2,394 71
Olmstead, Avery	978 00	515 74
Olmstead, Elizabeth,	1,322 00	733 02
Olmstead, James F	1,253 00	1,219 80
Olmstead, Julia M	2,398 00	1,179 70
O'Meara, John	350 00	313 00
Orman, Orris C	1,000 00	1,105 00
Osterhoudt, William	525 00	495 00
Ostrander, Mary J. S	3,057 56	Nothing
Ostrander, Mary J. S (reheard)	3,057 56	177 00

	Amount claimed.	Amount allowed.
Osborn, Hobart	$2,500 00	$767 14
Oswego Canal Co	40,000 00	9,645 50
Osborn, W. O.	1,010 00	703 50
Otto, August	45 00	Nothing
Otto, August (reheard)	45 00	45 00
Owen, B. (assignee of Downs & Gould)	2,350 00	2,262 00
Owen, Edward	64 50	Nothing
Owen, Edward (reheard)	64 50	64 00
Parker, John	450 00	100 00
Palmer, George W.	3,600 00	2,982 00
Paddock, John	7,050 00	5,821 44
Pardee, William J. (estate of)	4,081 46	1,900 00
Paine, Mary Ann	391 00	176 25
Paine, Thomas J.	150 00	100 00
Parshall, Amry	1,000 00	1,590 00
Parsons, James A.	760 00	580 00
Papke, Charles	419 37	60 00
Paddock, Simon D., Jr.	1,200 00	276 25
Patterson, Robert (trustee, &c.)	300 00	181 50
Pangburn, Charles	1,500 00	1,672 89
Palms, Anson P.	490 00	517 00
Patrick, Henry	3,150 00	3,701 25
Payne, Garrett W.	272 00	272 00
Paine, William H.	3,965 00	2,045 16
Park, Smith	2,245 00	939 36
Patterson, William	2,462 00	1,010 50
Pease, Ezra and Mary	750 00	400 00
Petrie, Adeline	175 00	Nothing
Petrie, Adeline (reheard)	175 00	175 00
Peck, Ira	12,485 00	4,529 48
Peck, Ira	5,000 00	1,926 00
Peck, Ira	3,000 00	2,599 20
Perry, John F.	2,000 00	750 00
Pettit, Louisa R.	31,816 00	15,743 54
Pearsall, William S.	3,031 00	2,788 28
Peck, George H.*	Not stated	2,534 48
Peterson & Hutchinson*	Not stated	3,500 00

	Amount claimed.	Amount allowed.
Peterson & Hosch, att'ys for C. F. Braman*	Not stated	$17,047 88
Phillips, Eliza	$1,500 00	860 00
Phelps, Ezekiel D	10,529 50	3,188 60
Pierce, Albert	1,500 00	1,000 00
Pierce, Elliot	1,200 00	1,048 00
Platner, Maria	1,000 00	500 00
Platt, Thomas C	6,141 50	4,697 30
Plumb, Ovid	3,496 00	3,187 50
Powell, Abner	525 00	Nothing
Porter & Weston	2,509 00	2,945 29
Post, Alanson	2,000 00	2,232 50
Potter, Joseph	5,695 47	3,500 00
Pruyn, John V. L	10,700 00	9,105 00
Presley, Harvey N	57 00	Nothing
Presley, Harvey N. (reheard)	57 00	57 00
Probasco, Samuel	2,930 00	973 56
Pulford, Samuel	3,000 00	1,200 00
Putnam, John L	3,000 00	1,326 00
Pumpelly, Frederick H. (estate of)	5,078 00	2,707 75
Quackenbush & Morrell	225 00	158 12
Ransom, Robert	2,800 00	100 00
Ray, Robert (trustee, &c.)	700 00	150 00
Rant, Patrick	2,000 00	1,382 52
Ray, Bannister & Co	7,244 50	884 00
Ramsey, Thomas	1,200 00	1,322 95
Ramsey, John A	4,500 00	1,200 00
Ray, Robert (trustee, &c.)	700 00	510 00
Rawson, Amon (executor of Edmund Rawson, deceased)	2,500 00	2,400 00
Ragan, Egbert	230 00	184 60
Ransom, Asa & Co.*	Not stated	120 00
Ray, James*	Not stated	7,500 00
Ranshaw, Mary	194 00	227 95
Ranshaw, Samuel B	278 00	176 25
Randall, Samuel A	2,762 00	1,434 67
Reese, William and others	4,500 00	1,394 64
Reese, Edwin	560 00	140 00

	Amount claimed.	Amount allowed.
Reese, Edwin	$560 00	$280 00
Rea, Walter	10,000 00	732 80
Reynold, Nathan	1,000 00	500 00
Reese, Anson	375 00	297 50
Regal, Charles	482 70	75 00
Reynolds, Oliver	500 00	396 00
Reed & Merrill, attorneys for D. & A. Z. Neff*	Not stated	15,069 94
Rhodes, Dexter	700 00	70 00
Rhodes, Charles*	Not stated	1,000 00
Rhodes, Mary J. (adm'x)	7,360 00	3,045 88
Rice, Augustus	7,645 80	5,454 00
Rice, Edwin	4,376 23	2,675 75
Rice, Levi	5,281 80	3,767 68
Rice, Luther	300 00	269 64
Rossell & Scrafford	240 00	120 00
Ross, William	800 00	630 00
Robinson, Robert	35,500 00	8,280 00
Robinson, Robert	35,500 00	15,306 66
Robinson, Robert & Sons	11,300 00	651 63
Robinson, Robert & Sons	2,968 40	2,736 00
Robinson, Robert & Sons	11,300 00	5,639 73
Rogers, Patrick	10,359 00	10,359 00
Roberts, Maria	1,500 00	1,383 35
Ross, Zebulon and E. P	5,000 00	2,000 00
Roberts, Maria	775 00	910 63
Robinson, William C	324 35	347 05
Root, Artemus	4,739 63	4,057 12
Rodman, Charles	2,425 00	1,677 28
Ross, George E. and Thomas J	6,060 00	2,420 50
Rose, Orrin W	1,750 00	2,331 87
Rumsey, Edwin S. and George	2,921 00	2,601 50
Rumsey, John A	4,500 00	3,300 00
Sands, Peter J	900 00	675 00
Sanders, Mary	100 00	50 00
Sanders, Garret	200 00	50 00
Sahr, Charles	1,600 34	300 00

	Amount claimed.	Amount allowed.
Sanford, Philip	$1,500 00	$1,489 20
Saddlemire, Catharine	1,500 00	1,649 13
Saddlemire, Paul	1,000 00	958 76
Scrafford, Christian	100 00	88 50
Schwinger, Christopher	2,000 00	1,281 39
Schermerhorn, Peter V. (estate of)	1,000 00	852 00
Schwinger, Rossina	1,500 00	497 66
Schoonmaker, Peter	500 00	Nothing
Scott, Walter	9,000 00	939 25
Schwinger, William	1,025 00	710 00
Schroeppel, Richard	3,000 00	1,635 32
Schroeppel, Mary (estate of)	1,200 00	287 86
Schab & Roreback*	Not stated	4,293 91
Schneider, Lewis*	Not stated	400 00
Scovill, Eaton & Mowry*	Not stated	3,352 48
Schneible, Paul	765 75	725 56
Seger, Laura E. and others	500 00	Nothing
Sekell, Loren	500 00	250 00
Seamans & Babcock	1,500 00	800 00
Sears, Odel M.	4,000 00	3,500 00
Seymour, Henry I.	6,848 40	1,819 40
Seelye, Lewis, assignee of B. M. Hanks*	Not stated	15,201 00
Seger, Laura E.	700 00	450 00
Seelye, Lewis*	Not stated	468 78
Seymour & Vernam*	Not stated	5,714 00
Seymour, Charles	4,772 50	4,046 43
Seaman, Horace	2,816 20	2,718 75
Shepard, Eli	500 00	125 00
Shepard, Joshua	150 00	120 00
Shepard, Harvey M.	500 00	200 00
Sharlock, Sarah	125 00	50 00
Shepard, Pratt	250 00	Nothing
Shepard, Pratt (reheard)	250 00	150 00
Sherman, George W.	500 00	340 00
Shoemaker, Andrew	1,311 00	Nothing
Shoemaker, Andrew (reheard)	1,311 00	1,311 00
Shell, Giles	8,691 16	1,140 00

	Amount claimed.	Amount allowed.
Shepard, Eli	$625 00	Nothing
Shepard, Elisha H. and others	8,640 00	$5,000 00
Shaub, Jacob*	Not stated	6,750 00
Shuts, John	820 00	963 50
Shuler, James D. (estate of)	5,000 00	3,350 00
Sheldon, Henry A.	3,069 50	1,409 88
Sherwood, Noah	2,000 00	1,116 66
Simmons, Elizabeth	652 00	652 00
Silsby, Horace C.	7,000 00	6,165 34
Simpson, John	573,52	443 00
Simpson, John	7,352 00	3,405 00
Simpson, John	1,100 00	229 50
Simpson, John	1,100 00	886 77
Sickles, Joseph	600 00	396 00
Silver, William	114 13	Nothing
Silver, William (reheard)	164 13	114 00
Sinclair, Frank A.	981 75	367 69
Skut, Hiram	375 00	Nothing
Skaneateles Iron Works	7,820 00	2,762 50
Skinner, Charles P.	1,150 00	969 00
Slocum, Arnold and others	Not stated	165 00
Slocum, Arnold, and Sally (executrix)	265 00	165 00
Seeper, Thomas C.	9,016 00	8,906 25
Smith, Royal Y.	7,055 00	1,807 15
Smith, Laban J.	6,015 00	2,656 67
Smith, Horace C.	575 00	675 63
Smith, Alonzo G.	1,455 00	1,656 75
Smith, Abigail	875 00	1,022 25
Smith, Russell*	Not stated	122 54
Smith, Lemuel and Hiram	10,000 00	1,846 67
Smith, Jedediah	250 00	132 60
Smith, Elizabeth	800 00	607 20
Smith, Elizabeth	600 00	85 00
Smith & Blaisdell	6,000 00	1,035 00
Smith, James D.	150 00	56 25
Smith, Roswell B.	5,000 00	4,969 28
Smith & Blaisdell	6,000 00	1,368 00

	Amount claimed.	Amount allowed.
Smith, Willis P.	$220 00	$165 75
Smith, Martha	2,000 00	406 60
Smith, George, and heirs of William Smith	8,750 00	6,524 00
Snyder, Frederick	1,500 00	1,360 00
Snook, Clark*	Not stated	302 87
Snook, Clark, attorney for Henry S. Pratt*	Not stated	10,521 21
Snook, Clark, assignee of Pratt & Candee*	Not stated	3,493 73
Snook & Beebe*	Not stated	40,000 00
Snyder, Joseph M.	1,712 00	856 00
Southard, Lester	1,000 00	902 56
Springsted, Jacob	350 00	100 00
Spencer, Margaret	508 00	Nothing
Spencer, Margaret (reheard)	508 00	400 00
Spencer, James D.	2,500 00	2,014 75
Spinner, Frances E.	550 00	550 00
Spaulding, Andrew*	Not stated	753 48
Spaulding, Andrew*	Not stated	7,682 60
Spaulding, Andrew*	Not stated	1,360 00
Sterling, John A.	908 96	908 96
Stearns, Josiah A.	3,192 40	3,065 62
Steel & Jennings	8,338 00	6,203 22
Steel, Aaron	2,892 50	1,820 50
Sterling, Daniel	105 75	75 00
Stone, James M.	125 00	75 00
Starr, Henry M. and Irvin M.	4,000 00	3,386 82
Stewart, Norman J.	400 00	399 00
Stebbins, Charles	500 00	50 00
Stevens, Chauncey	5,000 00	2,800 00
Stevenson, James M.	500 00	240 00
Strech, John	580 00	391 00
Strech, John	910 00	460 00
States, Patrick	437 00	228 44
Strum, Peter J.	175 00	157 29
Storrs, Francis A.	10,510 00	3,910 85
Stark, Elverton C.	600 00	705 00
Stanton, Samuel H.	350 00	181 90
Starbud, Charles*	Not stated	34 46

	Amount claimed.	Amount allowed.
Stephens, Clinton*	Not stated	$7,500 00
Susan, Henry	$1,310 00	Nothing
Susan, Henry (reheard)	1,310 00	235 00
Supervisors of Little Falls, and others	15,000 00	Nothing
Sumner, Alanson A	2,500 00	1,298 33
Sumner, Alanson A	1,000 00	460 00
Swan, Robert J	1,500 00	1,100 00
Sweeny, James, and others	1,500 00	1,100 00
Sweeny, James, and others	3,400 00	2,565 00
Swobe, Jacob	1,650 00	2,482 70
Syron, M. Coleman	500 00	90 00
Syron, Abraham B	500 00	100 00
Syron, M. Barton	500 00	440 00
Syracuse Peat and Marl Company	18,000 00	17,625 00
Talcott, Walter O	1,000 00	419 52
Taylor, Emily G	9,965 00	2,379 14
Tanner, C.*	Not stated	1,000 00
Terry, John G	800 00	Nothing
Thomas, Selah	160 00	160 00
Thomas, John T	660 00	331 50
Thurber, Frederick C	1,410 00	1,878 00
Thompson, Sophia R	285 00	251 45
Titus, David S	800 00	80 00
Tibbitts, Elizabeth	2,500 00	2,081 66
Tumey, Carlton K	7,800 00	749 00
Titcomb, Stephen	1,000 00	150 00
Tibbitts, Elizabeth	2,800 00	2,771 66
Torrey, Royal U	15,000 00	260 00
Torrey, Royal U	200 00	Nothing
Torrey, Royal U	10,000 00	Nothing
Torrey, Royal U	15,000 00	4,310 00
Torrey, Frank	9,000 00	5,138 50
Torrey, Frank	1,600 00	680 18
Tower, Julius C	480 00	Nothing
Tower, Julius C. (reheard)	480 00	180 00
Townsend, Justus and James H	6,000 00	4,000 00
Tremain, Cyrus S	290 00	340 75

	Amount claimed.	Amount allowed.
Tryon, Casper D.	$2,690 60	$2,445 00
Tripp, John	1,175 00	991 70
Traver, Martin	900 00	560 82
Travis, James	920 00	677 63
Treman & Banks	3,136 74	3,196 40
Tryon, William	845 00	711 65
Tuttle, Salmon	2,270 00	2,461 63
Tyler, Orrin	500 00	200 00
Ulerick, Martin	1,050 00	1,057 50
Van Cleef, William G.	1,800 00	187 50
Van Cleef, Johannah, and others	1,000 00	200 00
Van Aernam, Andrew J.	500 00	303 75
Van Kirk, Mary (heirs of)	800 00	563 00
Van Evera, Roof	92 50	90 48
Van Evera, Nicholas	686 00	381 00
Van Evera & Powers	280 00	242 34
Van Aernam, William C.	2,250 00	350 00
Van Wyck, Philip G.	2,800 00	672 40
Van Brocklin, Stephen A.	1,000 00	552 50
Van Nevery, William	1,500 00	50 00
Van Kirk, Betsey	2,000 00	1,500 00
Van Kirk, Amos	600 00	Nothing
Vandervoort, Mary F. (adm'x., &c.)	6,000 00	6,060 00
Vandervoort, William (estate of)	2,500 00	1,140 80
Vail, Mary B.	469 00	346 56
Van Benthuysen, John	8,020 00	5,043 51
Van Schryck, Elias	1,940 00	2,232 50
Vincent, Joshua	500 00	745 00
Vincent, Herbert B.	1,080 00	711 36
Voorhees, Peter	8,947 91	6,488 25
Voorhees, James L.	1,814 55	1,193 75
Walker, Peter	250 00	165 75
Wall, Theodocia	27,300 00	7,362 40
Waldruff, Peter	1,200 00	500 00
Ward & McVicar	8,625 00	5,721 52
Wager & Fales	49,758 21	13,969 30
Wasson, Elihu & Thos. T.	2,000 00	1,140 00

	Amount claimed.	Amount allowed.
Walker, Charles C. B.*	Not stated	$13,416 81
Ward & McVickar*	Not stated	1,570 00
Ward & McVickar, (assign. of J. G. Wood*)	Not stated	11,431 57
Watts, Margaret*	Not stated	1,500 00
West, Zelinda and others (exec. &c.)	$1,000 00	387 20
Wetherstone, Daniel	500 00	230 05
Weilman, Jacob	175 00	160 50
Wendt, William	612 18	218 00
Westbrook & Morehouse	500 00	200 00
Weeks, Hiram	2,730 00	2,891 52
Weed, Washington J	1,600 00	1,516 20
Wethey, Erastus	200 00	199 50
Weeks, Frederick	2,182 50	1,556 96
Weeks, Forrest G.	329 70	235 19
Wells, Charles	1,050 00	836 04
Webster, Lewis L.	2,050 00	1,144 58
Wheeler, Benedict & Co.	816 00	407 75
Wheeler, William J.*	Not stated	455 75
Whalen, Thomas	260 00	195 00
Wheeler, Eunice	157 00	Nothing
Wheeler, Eunice (reheard)	157 00	157 00
White, Truman M.	332 00	316 72
Wheeler, John	1,300 00	1,070 57
White, Nancy	100 00	85 00
Wheeler, Soloman	780 85	601 07
Wheeler, Isabella	1,000 00	806 54
White, Daniel	400 00	300 00
White, Amos C.	3,000 00	2,556 00
Whitehall Highway Com.*	Not stated	1,444 68
Whitney, Geo. J.*	Not stated	170 71
Whitcomb, Judah	3,772 00	3,231 25
White & Wait	1,582 50	1,735 48
Willard, Jacob G.	2,500 00	2,000 00
Wilkes, Martin F.	449 88	60 00
Wilkes, Michael	658 88	60 00
Williamson, Daniel R.	500 00	300 00
Willard, George W.	1,100 00	1,024 00

	Amount claimed.	Amount allowed.
Winans, Aaron (estate of.)	$1,000 00	$450 00
Winzor, Allen	150 00	130 00
Wilcox, Asel	750 00	Nothing
Wilson, James A.*	Not stated	19,454 75
Williams, Stephen	3,293 60	2,962 50
Willis, Benjamin and Riason	4,200 00	1,601 79
Wiggins, Alexander	115 00	124 84
Williams, Orrin P	370 00	434 75
Williams, Samuel	1,000 00	267 50
Wood, Alonzo & Son	3,220 00	663 00
Woodhull, Calvin	652 50	Nothing
Wooden, John H.*	Not stated	5,947 58
Wormley, John G	260 00	266 50
Writer, Gabriel W	5,115 00	2,185 81
Wright, Alice	1,401 60	120 00
Writers, Gabriel W	5,115 00	2,442 95
Wright, George A. Jr	1,080 00	1,092 75
Wurl, William	2,180 25	100 00
Wynant, Jacob	100 00	Nothing
Wynant, Jacob (reheard)	100 00	100 00
Yates, John	3,590 00	1,171 44
Yates, Daniel P. and William S	250 00	223 50
Youmans, Anthony	1,000 00	617 10
Young, William A	4,000 00	1,210 00
Yuille, ——	Not stated	314 00

CLAIMS PRESENTED

TO THE

CANAL BOARD AND CANAL APPRAISERS,

FROM SEPTEMBER 30TH, 1865, TO SEPTEMBER 30TH, 1870.

Names of claimants.	Amount claimed.
Abeel, Jacob	$1,610 00
Abele, Thomas	5,000 00
Abbott, Salmon	485 00
Abbott, Jeremiah E	4,318 00
Abrams, Mrs. Cordelia	3,000 00
Ackels, John	3,361 90
Ackerson, David	3,000 00
Adams, Joseph P	720 00
Adams & Close	25,000 00
Adams, Joseph P	48 15
Adams, Harry H	1,246 00
Adle, Joseph	500 00
Adle, Jacob	1,385 00
Adsit, Ansel M	941 00
Aileger, Thomas	679 50
Albany Pier Company	9,500 00
Alden, Walter S	160 00
Alden, Walter S	69 00
Aldrich, Benedict	1,085 66
Allen, Mrs. Nancy G	200 00
Allen & Burchard	1,177 57
Allen, William Y	100 00
Allen, Emory (assignee)	816 25
Amory, Rufus R	2,000 00
Anderson, George B	41,005 81
Anderson, John and George B	640 00

Names of claimants.	Amount claimed.
Angus, Charlotte	$652 00
Angus, John P	180 00
Anguish, Allen	1,480 00
Angel, Jacob	1,017 50
Armstrong, E. B	1,015 00
Armstrong, John and William	176 00
Arnold, Albert A	1,432 50
Art, Jacob	470 00
Arthur, Alfred	900 00
Ash, Thomas	410 00
Ash, Thomas	425 00
Ash, Thomas	93 50
Ashley, George	125 00
Ashley, George	475 00
Ashley, Nancy	750 00
Ashley, Jefferson	870 00
Austin, De Witt F	6,500 00
Ayer, Warren	2,996 00
Babcock, Henry H	702 18
Babcock & Peck	2,661 20
Babcock, William A	50 00
Bayley, George A. & E. Q. Senall	16,097 50
Bailey, Silas	2,000 00
Bailey, Franklin	100 00
Bailey, Harden	260 00
Baker, Lewis A	1,200 00
Baker, Roger	2,000 00
Babel, Jacob	320 75
Baker, Jonathan	885 50
Baker, Sarah	313 00
Balch, Eleanor	296 00
Ball, Eli and Martha D. & M. C. Felter	595 00
Ballard, Augustus	110 00
Ballon, Theodore P	12,000 00
Ballon, Theodore P	2,200 00
Baldwin, Irene S. (Loomis Baldwin, guardian,)	126 50
Baldwin, Lonson	485 75

Names of Claimants.	Amount claimed.
Baldwin, George W	$603 00
Balsley, Emily H	400 00
Bannister & Weeks	3,450 62
Banks, Alonzo	5,163 40
Barber, Joel	1,500 00
Barhydt, Nicholas	300 00
Barnes & Coleman	3,546 00
Barnes, Evert	1,000 00
Barnes, W. & J. W	460 00
Barnes, Eliza	55 00
Barker, Porter	160 00
Barron, Roger	750 00
Barrett, Stewart	375 00
Barry, Daniel	700 00
Barse, James	1,000 00
Barse, James	275 00
Barllette, G. H. & Frank Patrick	620 50
Bartholomew, Henry M	2,730 10
Bassett & Mills	5,000 03
Bassett, Norton	12,550 00
Bassett, Norton	4,098 95
Batt, John	1,500 00
Bath, John	3,000 00
Baty, Ransom	1,529 50
Bayer, Mrs. E	121 00
Bayer, Jacob G	180 00
Bayer, Jacob B	75 00
Bayer, Henry	455 00
Bayer, Andrew	173 63
Baggard, Francis	1,555 00
Beach, Nelson J	1,000 00
Beach, Nelson J	100 00
Beach, Nelson J	211 88
Beach, Ralph, Jr	4,050 00
Beadle, Laomini, Jr	2,000 00
Bear, John	2,273 00
Beard, Nelly M	180 00

Names of Claimants.	Amount claimed.
Beecher, Hamilton	$2,250 00
Beecher, Hamilton	750 00
Becker, Martin	1,000 00
Becker, Levi	1,310 50
Becker, George	490 00
Beckwith, Hannah (committee of)	400 00
Behm, Charles	3,668 00
Belden, A. Cadwell	2,000 00
Belling, Charles	705 00
Belling, Charles	124 50
Benedict, George	1,000 00
Benedict, Wheeler & Co	816 00
Bender, Wendell M., Son & Co	2,081 58
Benjamin, Allen	1,704 00
Bennet, Roswell G	3,286 00
Bennet, Benjamin F	1,200 00
Bennett, Gennett	650 00
Bennett, William	3,447 00
Bennage, Andrew	231 00
Benson, Benjamin	2,820 00
Benthin, Augustus	590 00
Bentin, Christian	555 00
Berger, John	2,000 00
Betsinger, Hezekiah	2,760 50
Bettinger, John	3,000 00
Betts, Orry	355 00
Betts, Ira	1,547 00
Betts, Ira	21,500 00
Betts, Ira (executor, &c.)	3,750 00
Bibbins, Samuel	1,148 00
Billington, Charles	1,000 00
Billinghurst, Lucien	276 00
Binninger, H	475 00
Binninger & Strainge	550 00
Binsse, Anna M.	560 00
Birdsall, Ausburn	5,000 00
Bissel, Augustus H.	1,537 50

Names of Claimants.	Amount claimed.
Bissell, Charlotte (estate of Walter Bissell, deceased)	$3,548 70
Bissell, Andrew H.	1,218 00
Bissell, Edwin B.	3,750 00
Bishop, John	600 00
Blake, Anson, Jr. (and others, executors)	1,055 00
Blakeman, George T.	1,000 00
Blasdell, John C.	230 00
Blasdell, John C.	2,000 00
Blasdell, John C.	885 00
Bliss, Seth P.	1,960 91
Blodgett, Andrew	75 00
Blodgett, Andrew	376 00
Blood, Joel	1,390 43
Blood, Robert	1,000 00
Blood, Robert	1,000 00
Blood, John D.	5,830 00
Bloodgood, Winfield	3,695 00
Bloodgood, Mrs. Mary	25,000 00
Blossom, Christopher W.	90 00
Booneville (town of),	3,900 00
Booth, Harvey	2,665 00
Boots, John	830 00
Bordwell, William	314 95
Boshart, Charles D.	232 00
Botsford, Augustus	2,176 26
Boshart, James H.	189 50
Boughton, Peter	1,000 00
Bourke, Patrick	500 00
Bowen, Alonzo	329 70
Bowman, Jacob	1,200 00
Boyer, Phillip	527 50
Boyer, Phillip	39 00
Boyle, Barney	400 00
Bradley, S. W.	1,000 00
Bradshaw, Joseph	640 00
Bradt, Francis and John	535 00
Bradt, Abraham M.	750 00

Names of Claimants.	Amount claimed.
Branaugh, Samuel	$3,861 00
Brandt, William	90 00
Brant, Hiram	180 00
Braitmayer, John G.	200 00
Breason, John	342 50
Bredo, John	1,205 00
Bremer, Frederick	800 00
Brennan, James	1,000 00
Brennan, Emily	15,000 00
Brett, Delos & S. Brett	6,780 00
Briggs, Hiram S.	1,121 00
Briggs, Noah	2,146 50
Brigham, Samuel	180 00
Brigham, Sullivan	1,100 00
Brigham, Louisa	1,200 00
Brisbin, D. C.	600 00
Bronson, Eli A.	756 90
Brooks, David	1,000 00
Broomhall, Henry	1,300 00
Brown, Isaac F.	1,662 00
Brown, George	1,368 00
Brown, George W.	602 00
Brown, Caleb	648 00
Brown, Sarah and C. P. Ryther	1,982 00
Brown, Edward, (assignee, &c.)	1,950 00
Brown, Nancy	550 00
Brown, Edwin D	420 00
Brownell, Clinton D.	1,300 00
Brownville and Pamelia Plank Road Co	158 67
Brougham, John H.	1,000 00
Bruining, Wilhelm	1,967 00
Bruon, Henry	250 00
Bruon, Henry	280 00
Buck, Edwin	175 00
Buckingham, Mary	100 00
Buckley, Patrick	973 00
Buckley, Patrick	407 50

Names of Claimants.	Amount claimed.
Buckley, Patrick	$900 00
Buckley, Patrick	500 00
Buckley, Patrick	150 00
Buckley, Timothy	245 00
Bugh, Henry	221 00
Bull, Joseph	1,246 25
Bullar, John	410 00
Bullard, George W	455 00
Burdick, Albert	802 40
Burdick, James	500 00
Burdick, Matthew T	6,150 00
Burdick, Henry	780 00
Burdick, S. Edgar	460 00
Burk, James	1,750 00
Burk, Francis	1,750 00
Burk, Hiram L	1,750 00
Burke, Thomas	1,500 00
Burfeerd, Henry	830 00
Burlingame, Linus	1,015 00
Burlingame, Francis	145 00
Burroughs, Silas	369 20
Burne, Adelbert	3,025 00
Burne, Percy	150 00
Burnett, William H	300 00
Burnett, A. Jay	500 00
Burns, John	160 00
Burr, Charles A	128 00
Burr, Miranda C	360 00
Burrows, Roswell S	25,000 00
Burt, Ira	400 00
Burton, Benjamin	4,135 00
Bush, Alfred	700 00
Butterfield, Oliver (estate of)	625 00
Butterfield, Duane et al	950 00
Butterfield, Oliver	330 00
Butts, Martin	1,200 00
Buta, Charles	2,304 00

Names of Claimants.	Amount claimed.
Byrne, Michael	$150 00
Byrnes, Daniel	1,500 00
Byrns, Edward	1,300 00
Cagney, Sarah	1,200 00
Camp, James F	2,264 00
Camp, James F	5,070 00
Camp, Roswell	1,295 00
Campbell, John G	3,000 00
Campbell, Aley	3,000 00
Campbell, Conley, E	2,106 27
Campbell & Thompson	150 00
Canada, Minerva	200 00
Candee, Charles W. (guardian, &c.)	2,200 00
Candee, Charles W. & Gay Candee	2,200 00
Candee, Charles W	3,000 00
Cannon, George	100 00
Card, Daniel	1,100 00
Carey, Rody	235 50
Carye, Rody	115 00
Cary, Andrew	1,070 00
Carney, James	700 00
Carney, James	1,154 00
Carney, James	348 00
Carney, Henry	1,399 50
Carney, Horace	1,045 00
Carney, Horace	813 00
Carnochan, Mary	1,478 00
Carlton, Fanny E. (adm'x. of Orville N. Carlton)	710 00
Carter, George	180 00
Carter, George	275 00
Carter, Hiram	120 00
Carter, Emily	450 00
Carter, E. C.	3,000 00
Carterton, Thomas	1,700 00
Case, John	1,525 00
Case, Lorenzo	1,543 00
Case, Lorenzo and E. C. Case	2,940 18

Names of Claimants.	Amount claimed.
Case, William H.	$550 00
Casey, Patrick	250 00
Catlin, Jacob F.	7,590 00
Catlin, Nathaniel	2,710 00
Catlin, Nicholas M.	410 00
Catlin, Nicholas M.	101 50
Cayuga and Seneca Bridge Co.	3,000 00
Chadwick, John	1,713 65
Chadwick, Holland W.	1,500 00
Chadwick, William	429 00
Chaffee, Norman J.	3,000 00
Chamberlain, Calvin F.	13,000 00
Chamberlain, Calvin T.	13,000 00
Chamberlain, Cornelius G.	1,275 00
Chamberlain, Hazen	5,000 00
Chamberlain, J. P. (assignee, &c.)	3,644 43
Chamberlain, Ira A.	138 00
Champlain, M. B.	300 00
Champlin, Jabez	1,585 00
Champlin, Jab.z	1,000 00
Chaphy, Lucy	500 00
Chapman, John R.	975 00
Chapman, John R.	1,000 00
Cheever, Samuel	1,000 00
Chesbro, Martin	3,600 00
Chrisman, William	1,290 00
Christ, Joseph	324 00
Churchill, William	12,208 80
Churchill, Ward	1,134 10
Churchill, Peter	3,693 50
City of Syracuse	4,280 00
Clapp, James H.	737 00
Clapper, Enoch	100 00
Clark, Linus R.	12,002 50
Clark, Reuben P.	486 00
Clark, Stephen, et al. (committee)	5,874 00
Clark, Wheeler H. and Edward	300 00

Names of Claimants.	Amount claimed.
Clark, Wheeler H	$1,857 00
Clark & Little	273 00
Clark, George	349 80
Clarke, Erskine G	1,460 00
Clements, Jane	270 00
Cleveland, Jerome	662 50
Cleveland, Pascal H	425 00
Cleveland, Philander	202 50
Cleveland, U. A	1,130 00
Cleveland, Uriah A. (executor, &c)	2,800 00
Clifford, Richard	3,480 00
Clinton, Elizabeth	1,017 00
Close, S. H. & S. B. Adams	10,322 50
Clapman, Lydia H	200 00
Cobb, Roxanna	200 00
Coburn, William M	2,095 00
Coburn, Andrew and Ebenezer	2,550 00
Codman, Gustavus	429 76
Coe, Curtis	250 00
Coe, Dennis M	178 42
Coe, Samuel N	1,610 00
Cogswell, George F	762 00
Cole, Byron & Charles H. Steele	775 00
Cole, Samuel J	4,025 00
Cole, Ambrose F	184 50
Coleman, William	229 50
Coleman, William	680 00
Coleman, Robert S	632 50
Coleman, Robert S	200 00
Coleman, Obadiah	675 00
Collins, Charles	5,000 00
Collins, Charles	6,000 00
Collins, Richard	300 00
Commissioners Highways Town of Portville	3,000 00
Commissioners of Highways	1,500 50
Commissioners of Highways	421 50
Commissioners of Highways	675 00

Names of Claimants.	Amount claimed.
Commissioners of Highways	$749 70
Compson, Stephen	300 00
Conklin, Timothy	500 00
Conklin, T. J. & Co	36,645 40
Conant, Samuel H	7,701 62
Congdon, Allen	67 50
Congdon, Allen	160 00
Connors, Patrick	900 00
Cony, Reuben	900 00
Connihan, Catherine	460 00
Conrad, Henry J	208 00
Conroy, Charles	4,525 00
Conroy, Charles	4,855 00
Cook, Sarah M	600 00
Cook, Andrus	3,300 00
Cook, Joseph I	2,500 00
Cookingham, Peter	1,000 00
Cookingham, Peter	1,500 00
Cooley, Rosanna	360 00
Coonrad, Peter	1,936 00
Cooper, George and Samuel	4,080 00
Cooper, William J	480 00
Cooney, Patrick	3,000 00
Cooney, Nicholas	8,000 00
Copeland, William	200 00
Corinne, G. W. & N. Soule	2,500 00
Coston, Charles C	1,318 36
Covell, George W	1,945 00
Covell, Stephen A	520 00
Covell, J. D	600 00
Cagger, Peter	7,500 00
Craine, Almond W. & Perry P	5,000 00
Crainer, George W	985 00
Crandell, Enos S	2,950 00
Crandell, L. W	2,247 00
Crandell, George	545 00
Crandell, Warren	1,400 00

Names of Claimants.	Amount claimed.
Crandell, Warren & W. S. Potter	$1,500 00
Crandell, Warren & W. S. Potter	3,200 00
Crandell, Warren & W. S. Potter	200 00
Crandle, R. S. & Seth Crandle	700 00
Crandle, Seth	350 00
Crandle, Richard S	500 00
Crane, George	225 00
Crawford, Harry	156 00
Crawford, Joseph	900 00
Crocker, C. R	220 00
Cross, J. C. et al	300 00
Crossman & Force	3,000 00
Crownhart, Henry	1,500 00
Crowley, Timothy	425 00
Crowley, Timothy	44 50
Crysler, Martin	2,000 00
Curley, Furgus	245 00
Curley, Furgus	243 00
Curtis, Alonzo	200 00
Curtis, Charles H	60 00
Cushing, T. C. and A. A	1,500 00
Custer & Flynn	20,489 13
Cutler, Stillman	572 50
Cuyler, George N	7,540 00
Daggett, Mrs. Mary E.	1,000 00
Daggert, Jonathan	350 00
Daily, John	425 00
Daley, Terence	390 00
Daley, Terence	815 00
Daley, Terence	832 00
Daley, John	2,447 48
Dalton, James	300 00
Daliarmie, Theobold	6,060 00
Daly, Bryan	960 00
Daly, Bryan	63 00
Damon, Clark	350 00
Damon, Norton J	1,000 00

Names of Claimants.	Amount claimed.
Dann, Horace S.	$3,756 50
Daniels, Amos	4,185 00
Daniels, Amos R.	325 00
Darron, John B.	660 00
Davidson, George	100 00
Davidson, Josiah L.	2,062 00
Davis, Jonathan	4,250 00
Davis, John A.	2,034 75
Davis, Aaron C.	180 00
Davis, Alonzo	2,000 00
Davis, Alonzo	1,500 00
Davison, John	140 00
Dean, William	1,274 20
Deforest, Schuyler	700 00
Deforest, Schuyler	661 00
De Graff, Gilbert	300 00
De Groat, Lorenzo M.	1,100 00
Deger, John G.	1,515 00
Deihl, John	1,612 50
Delaney, Patrick P.	500 00
Demont, George	500 00
Demont, William	750 00
Deney, Cadwell	26,900 00
Deney, Cadwell	1,400 00
Denio, Salena	2,230 00
Denio, Benjamin F.	425 00
Denio, Benjamin F.	425 00
Dennis, Nicholas	367 00
Dennison, B. A.	700 00
Denniston, Dewitt C.	770 00
Denslow, Gould	215 00
Devendorf, Cornelius V.	210 00
Devereaux, Albert	4,000 00
Devereaux, Patrick	1,546 00
Devereaux, Patrick	810 00
Dewey, C. D.	3,899 50
Dewey, Asahel P.	400 00

Names of Claimants.	Amount claimed.
Dexter, David	$3,500 00
Dexter, David	404 00
Dexter, David & Son	100 00
Dibble, Horace	1,005 00
Dibble, Le Roy A.	55 85
Dickerson & Kennedy	5,200 00
Dickerson & Kennedy	10,486 12
Dickerman, H. H., & S. S. Hoyt	22,274 42
Diefendorf, Catharine	7,450 00
Disbrow, Catharine	744 05
Dixon, James	2,150 00
Dixon & White	4,000 00
Dodge, Harvey	500 00
Dodge, Byron	187 50
Doonan, James	750 00
Dornfeld, Albert	1,460 00
Dornfeld, William	221 75
Dougherty, Samuel	1,500 00
Douglas, Ansel C.	410 00
Downs, Abel, and S. S. Gould (assignee of)	2,175 00
Drake, Jane E	300 00
Drummond, William	180 00
Dubois, George	745 00
Dudley, George F.	450 00
Dudley, G. F.	289 44
Dumsie, Michael	200 00
Dunn, Margaret	1,600 00
Dunkin, Aaron W	497 50
Dunkleburger, Mrs. Caroline	1,550 00
Dunham, Valentine	8,000 00
Dunlap, Eliza W.	2,000 00
Dunn, John	1,000 00
Dunn, Thomas	300 00
Dwyer, John	277 50
Dyer, Barton H.	945 00
Eacker, William E	1,825 00
Eagan, Charles	95 50

Names of Claimants.	Amount claimed.
Eames Moses et al. (dam owners)	$3,000 00
Eames, Frances A. and J. Augustus Eames	1,050 00
Eames, Moses	873 60
Eames, Moses & E. W. Morgan	3,000 00
Earlls & Tallman	1,457 22
Earlls, Thayer & Co	6,320 43
Earlls, Thayer & Co	8,152 88
Earlls & Tallman	1,457 22
Earll, A. J.	532 00
Earll, George H. & Co	835 00
Earll, S. H. & Co	375 00
Earls, A. J. & A. Boughton	210 00
Eastbrooks, John A.	2,200 00
Eastman, John R. (agt. of Lucy Ann Eastman)	237 20
Eberly, Mattice	564 00
Eddy, Sarah A	512 00
Edgar, William H	679 02
Edgerton, Daniel	466 00
Edgerton, R. H.	2,000 00
Edwards, Hiram K	975 00
Edwards, John	377 40
Edin, John	280 00
Eggleston, John	2,500 00
Ehrenwick, Christ.	987 00
Eldredge, Margaret	2,569 00
Eldredge, Loren R. and Lewis	3,652 00
Eldredge, Ann E. and children	12,500 00
Eli, Edward O	4,100 00
Ellis, Charles A	775 00
Ellis, Charles W.	699 00
Ellis Joseph F.	502 00
Ely, Ann S.	7,500 00
Emerson, Philip	225 00
Emerson, John	45 00
Emerson, Frederick	62 13
Emmons, John W.	150 00
Emmons, Edward N.	200 00

Names of Claimants.	Amount claimed.
Emmons, Samuel	$300 00
Emmons, Harriet	150 00
Enders, Jacob H.	100 00
Enders, Jacob H., & Catharine E. Voorhes	950 00
Enders, Peter	5,717 25
Enders, Peter, & Catharine Ann Voorhes	3,163 00
Evans, William V.	1,000 00
Evans, Evan, and James Evans	
Evans, William	2,585 92
Everts, W. A. & E. R. Evans	1,806 00
Francher, Ira, Jr.	2,000 00
Fancher, Idas	500 00
Farnell, Addison M., & Co.	15,953 31
Farr, Jason	436 58
Farr, Jason	7,300 00
Farr, Jason	4,100 00
Farr, Alvin	4,100 00
Farrar, Harvey D.	216 50
Farwell, Abram	200 00
Favor, John	10,000 00
Fayle, Thomas	2,500 00
Feltman, John C.	2,056 39
Felter, Darwin	540 00
Fenton, John	2,600 00
Ferguson, Mary A.	1,129 00
Ferris, Benjamin	670 00
Ferris, Charles	595 00
Figel, Joseph	150 00
Filmer, James	1,235 00
Finley, N. S., & E. Parton	232 50
Fineour, John	1,200 00
Fisher, H. E.	1,000 00
Fischer, Theobold	1,095 00
Fisher, James, and others	1,500 00
Fisk, John M.	1,207 00
Fitch, Orson	36 00
Fitzgerald, George, & Martin Kane	300 00

Names of Claimants.	Amount claimed.
Fitzer, George	$159 00
Fletcher, Wentworth & Co	4,380 00
Flood, Jeremiah	1,250 00
Flynn, Jane and James	360 00
Flynn, Jane and Mary Jane	1,930 00
Foland, Jonas	2,365 00
Forest Port Lumber and Slate Manufacturing Co	2,654 50
Ford, Joseph K	1,200 00
Fort Edwards Water Works Co	800 00
Foster, Alban	3,500 00
Foster, David	550 00
Foster, Owen S	2,097 86
Fowler, Joseph	160 00
Fox, Mrs. Olivia	1,625 00
Fraser, Charles E	1,600 00
Frazier, Barbara M	320 00
Freeman, Pattison	1,600 00
French, Albert G	4,536 00
Frink, Charles G	22,600 00
Fritz, William	831 42
Fritz, William	412 50
Fritsche, Ferdinand	469 00
Frize, Jacob	752 50
Fronty, Jacob	2,000 00
Frost, Abial	537 50
Frost, James	2,800 00
Fry, John	453 50
Fuller, David H	4,908 50
Fuller, Darwin	625 00
Fuller, Joseph	1,350 00
Fuller & Mannering	6,000 00
Fulton, John (guardian et al.)	300 00
Gage, George	500 00
Gale, Thomas	2,475 00
Gale, Thomas & Co	1,500 0
Gallagher, Thomas	945 0
Gallagher, James	23,925 0

Names of Claimants.	Amount claimed.
Gallagher, John	$525 00
Galvin, John	200 00
Gande, John	185 00
Gardner, Egbert	100 00
Gates, Archibald H	9,703 45
Gates, Linus M	280 00
Gay, Edward	400 00
Gay, Edward	460 00
Gay, Stephen	186 00
Gere, Isaac W	24,700 00
George, Henry and others	800 00
Gerhard, Martin, Jr	495 00
Getman, Thomas	537 00
Gifford, Cordelia	1,044 00
Gifford, Cordelia C	2,500 00
Gilchrist, James H	1,457 00
Gillmartin, James and Winneford	1,200 00
Gill, Lucius	927 22
Gillespie, W. C	1,455 92
Gillett & Clark	1,671 00
Glann, George and James H	3,731 00
Glass, Breed & Co	10,000 00
Glass, Breed & Co	21,000 00
Glann, William	5,655 00
Glassgow, Ralph	500 00
Gleason, Sanford	1,750 00
Goff, William	1,879 29
Goodale, Lawrence J	199 50
Goodman, Christopher	445 00
Goodrich, Edwin	2,543 00
Goodrich, George W., (sec'y &c.)	6,916 00
Goodspeed, Joel J	11,300 00
Goodwin, Samuel	800 00
Gordon, Fordyce F	182 50
Gould, George	2,000 00
Gould, Samuel A	1,000 00
Gould, Samuel A	2,500 00

Names of Claimants.	Amount claimed.
Graff, Philip	$4,400 00
Graff, John	158 50
Graff, John	450 00
Graff, Jacob	687 50
Graham, John	100 00
Grassman, William	926 00
Gratten, Patrick	7,040 00
Graves, Thomas J	400 00
Graves, Thomas J	400 00
Graves, Nathan	225 00
Gray, John C	150 00
Green, Charles H	435 00
Green, Job J	14,385 00
Greenleaf, Susan	400 00
Great Bend Paper Company	957 50
Griffin, Alfred E	1,400 00
Griffin, Shimuel	1,000 00
Griffin, Orrin	3,699 05
Griffin, Erastus W	100 00
Griffith, Evans & Co	8,015 00
Grinnell, Seymour	390 00
Griswold, William L	884 00
Groesbeck, Isaac W	1,220 00
Groesbeck, Isaac W	1,960 00
Groesbeck, Cornelius	2,940 00
Groeskopf, Frederick	1,315 00
Groeskopf, Christine	5,711 00
Groeskopf, Henry	300 00
Grotenwalt, Charlotte	1,710 00
Groundrill, William	860 20
Guardinier James and Cornelius	170 00
Guarin, David	820 00
Guarin, Daniel	108 50
Guarin, Daniel	220 00
Guarin, Daniel	520 00
Guarin, James	645 00
Guarin, James	700 00

Names of Claimants.	Amount claimed.
Guile, Betsey	$53 25
Guilford, Charles	1,208 70
Gullret, Frank	3,000 00
Gunther, Henry	75 00
Gurnee, Albert	450 00
Gutches, Margaret E	1,000 00
Guyot, Minor and J. V. Guyot	120 00
Hadcock, Solomon	3,391 30
Hagadorn, Sylvanus	259 00
Haggerty, John	2,372 91
Hahee, William	90 00
Haight, Maria	1,500 00
Hale, Francis Hammond	2,258 00
Halley, George	150 00
Halpin, Christopher	400 00
Hall, John H	103 35
Hall, Mary E	800 00
Hall, Samuel A	3,000 00
Hall, Antoine	4,000 00
Hall, Franklin J., (agt. for water power owners)	350 00
Hall and Maltby	2,044 00
Halsey, Luther H	500 00
Hammond, Charles	429 00
Hanchett and Delong	5,000 00
Hand, Jacob et al	9,410 00
Hannay, Alexander	200 00
Hannegan, Thomas	1,500 00
Harbeck, Elijah S. and John	5,712 00
Harden, Laura	600 00
Harden, Samuel H	315 00
Harder, John H	375 00
Harder, Peter	2,050 00
Harding, Lowell	3,500 00
Hardy, M. W	505 00
Hardy, Lyman B	4,000 00
Hardy, Henry	4,220 00
Haich, Charles	330 00

Names of Claimants.	Amount claimed.
Hardy, Stephen	$333 25
Hardy, Susan	145 00
Harford, George	455 00
Harrigan, Thomas	1,200 00
Harrigan, Thomas	1,500 00
Harrington, Richard D	4,850 00
Harrington, Robert H	484 00
Harris, Nathaniel	93 00
Harris, Henry	1,561 00
Harris, Esther	577 00
Harris, Joseph H	75 00
Harris, Joseph H	819 50
Hart, Amasa P	21,250 00
Hart, Amasa P	13,650 00
Hart, George	269 00
Harter, Peter	100 00
Hartford, George	427 50
Harvey, John	8,078 50
Harvey, Ann	440 00
Harvey, George	420 00
Harvey, George	770 00
Harvey, George	1,250 00
Harvey, George	765 00
Harvey, David	555 00
Harvey, David	485 00
Harvey, David	238 75
Haskins, James P	Not stated
Haskins, Linus S	1,790 00
Hatch, Junius H	475 00
Hatch, Catharine	1,250 00
Hathaway, James	1,100 00
Hathaway, John M	180 00
Hawley, Thomas	400 00
Hawley, Alonzo	5,000 00
Hawn, John W	2,320 00
Hawthorne, Robert	300 00
Hayden, Charles, and others	15,240 00

Names of Claimants.	Amount claimed.
Hayden, Charles, and others	$72,000 00
Hayden, Ezra, and others	2,800 00
Hayden, Julia	825 00
Hayes, Simeon	340 00
Hazen, Mary H	200 00
Heit, George	1,000 00
Heitz, Philip	156 67
Helmer, David	600 00
Helmer, Gilbert W	214 30
Hendricks, George	5,000 00
Hendrix, James	308 00
Hennesey, Mary	890 00
Hennesey, Michael	75 00
Hennesey, Margaret et al	1,000 00
Henry, Mary	1,337 50
Henry, Mary	735 00
Henry, William	987 50
Henry, William	990 00
Heustis, Ephraim P	200 00
Herrick, A. H., & J. P. Moulton	9,331 00
Hess, Archibald	1,200 00
Hess, Frederick	105 00
Hickel, Michael, & William H. Vickers	300 00
Hicks, Alanson	10,707 00
Hicks, Edward	1,620 00
Higby, Curtis	274 00
Higginbothan, Sands	750 00
Higher, Michael	298 00
Hill, Timothy	1,925 00
Hill, Hiram	1,150 00
Hill, Samuel	425 00
Hilt, Sally	152 50
Hillyer, Myron	3,419 15
Hinman, Mary	345 00
Histed, George S	3,935 00
Histed, Rensselaer	1,001 25
Hitchcock, Albert	292 50

Names of Claimants.	Amount claimed.
Hitchcock, Chester	$508 00
Hoadley, Leonard	5,000 00
Hoard, Charles B	1,110 00
Hodgkins, Ezra	535 04
Hodgkins, B. F. and John L	4,300 80
Hoessle, Jacob R	7,860 00
Hoffman, Gotlieb	552 00
Holcomb, Hiram	1,211 67
Hollister, Jesse	200 00
Hollister, William, & John D. Fay	17,605 00
Holler, John	1,752 50
Holler, Nicholas	2,492 00
Holmes, John	3,490 00
Holmes, Albert	65 00
Holton, Thomas	600 00
Holway, Ellen	1,055 00
Hooke, Mathias	7,587 00
Hosfeld, Frederick*	295 84
Hopkins, George	1,600 00
Hopkins, John W. and Nancy	300 00
Hopkins, John W.	400 00
Hopkins, Samuel C	130 00
Hopper, James	500 00
Hopper, Norman	400 00
Horan, Patrick	3,375 00
Horton, Harriet J	4,000 00
Horton, Michael	800 00
Horton, Wilson and John B	300 00
Hotchkiss, George	730 00
Houck, George	150 00
Housel, Israel P	909 90
Howell, Edwin W	1,367 12
Howell, Stephen W	1,307 09
Howell, Lewis B	8,000 00
Howes, Enoch	300 00
Howland, Robert B	10,100 00
Howland, Phœbe Jane	7,800 00

Names of Claimants.	Amount claimed.
Hoyt, E. B	$1,309 00
Hoyt, E. B. and Jane	200 00
Hubbard, Daniel	2,300 00
Hubbard, Daniel	3,290 00
Hubbard, Daniel	492 52
Hubbard, Daniel	210 00
Hubbard, William O	5,000 00
Hubbard, William O	12,569 97
Hubbard, J. B. & Charles North	675 11
Hubbard, Mary B	1,000 00
Hudson, Edward	5,000 00
Hudson, Boyd R	9,725 00
Hughson, John	1,002 00
Hughson, Lorenzo D	3,048 30
Hulburt, Lewis B	525 00
Hulbert, John W	15,000 00
Hulbert, Angelica V. R	4,500 00
Hulbert, J. P. (heirs and executors of)	10,000 00
Hull, Mrs. Rhoda	350 00
Humsicker, E	500 00
Humsicker, E	1,000 00
Hunt, Seth	8,250 00
Hunt, Aaron B	1,550 00
Hunter, Thomas S	7,817 50
Hunt, Aaron B. and Daniel F	4,800 00
Hunter, Jane	100 00
Huntington, Joseph	2,075 00
Huntington, C. S. & G. W. Pennock	1,600 00
Hurd, George	500 00
Hyland & Evans	5,000 00
Ide, Henry, Jr	675 00
Ingalls, George F	320 00
Ingalls, George S	560 00
Ingalls, George S	770 00
Ingalls, Aaron	1,125 80
Ingalls, John	33 00
Ingersoll, Charles	644 00

Names of Claimants.	Amount claimed.
Ingerson, Daniel	$2,000 00
Ives, Francis	57 00
Ives, Garret	60 00
Jacobie, William H	270 00
Jacobs, D. C	6,097 73
Jacobs, James P	500 00
Jewett, Charles G. & Eli C. Hines	900 00
Jewett, Maurice	160 00
Johnson, Jefferson	810 00
Johnson, William P	1,000 00
Johnston, James	645 00
Johnston, James	600 00
Johnston, Henry	1,000 00
Johnston, Sarah E	175 00
Johnston, Francis & G. M. Gilbert	675 00
Johnston, Timothy B	1,582 25
Johnston, Walter	300 00
Jones, David E	1,715 00
Jones, John R	545 00
Jordon, James O	1,775 00
Joslin, Hosea F	180 00
Kasten, John H	1,290 00
Keane, Nicholas	600 00
Kearney, John D	10,900 00
Keefe, Daniel	800 00
Kellawald, William	277 00
Kelly, Catherine et al	1,000 00
Kelly, Isaac	759 92
Kelly, William	175 00
Kelly, Patrick, deceased (widow and heirs of)	200 00
Kendrick, Mariah	2,500 00
Kendrick, Mariah	25,000 00
Kent, Isaac	304 00
Kent, Isaac	1,000 00
Kent, Phineas & John E. Andrus	760 00
Kepp, Frederick	266 00
Ketchum, L. S	2,000 00

Names of Claimants.	Amount claimed.
Ketchum, L. S.	$900 00
Keyes, William	1,000 00
Kibber, Christ	1,789 00
Kibber, George	2,110 00
Kibber, George, Jr	216 00
Kibber, Margaret	281 00
Kibber, Rick	1,055 00
Kidder, George C	490 00
Kimball, Volney P	12,132 00
Kimball, Jacob	4,190 00
Kincaid, Alexander	1,200 00
Kincaid, Alexander	900 80
Kingsbury, John (heirs of)	3,781 20
Kinne, Erastus M	169 00
Kinney, Henry	1,506 50
Kinney, Warren	716 40
Kinney, Phineas Z. and Elizabeth, executors, &c	1,500 00
Kinyon, Willis E.. David Dorrance	1,484 00
Kirkland, Susan B	1,110 00
Kirkpatrick, David	266 60
Kirby, William P	2,500 00
Kitts, Henry	270 00
Kittrick, James	1,500 00
Kittrick, John	400 00
Klein, Adam	736 00
Klingenschmidt, Henry A	145 00
Klidgenschmidt, Andrew	707 00
Kladler, Frederick	4,640 00
Knapp, Erastus	400 00
Knowlton, J. C. and G. W	5,800 00
Knowlton, J. C. and G. W. & J. H. Rice	300 00
Knowlton, J. C. and others	3,000 00
Koch, Martin	730 00
Koch, Robert L	318 00
Kohlu, David	1,160 00
Kohler, Christopher	772 50
Kohler, David and Charles	2,849 24

Names of Claimants.	Amount claimed.
Krall, William	$826 00
Kreig, Philip	1,105 50
Kribbel, Mary	623 50
Kroning, Augustus	215 00
Krull, William	243 75
Ladd, Shuball	437 50
La Fever, Maria L	120 00
Lafferty, Hugh	740 00
La Grange, Laura, et al.	3,330 00
La Grange, Moses	1,980 00
La Grange, Willam A	400 00
Lamb, Robert	1,648 00
Lamb, William E	160 00
Lamb, Chauncy B	250 00
La Mont, Frederick S.	2,244 00
La Monte, Daniel M	2,712 00
La Mount, Samuel	5,160 00
Lamphear, Kendrid	241 00
Lane, Amos	3,520 00
Lane, Chauncy	Not stated
Lane, Peter B.	919 50
Lanther, John	675 00
Lappeus, Henry (amended claim)	700 00
Larabee, Hamilton R. and Alvin	1,000 00
Laraway, Catharine M.	250 00
Laraway, George, & R. B. Eaker	6,000,00
Laikins, Timothy	1,500 00
Larzerlere, H. M. and H. W	1,000 00
Laton, Jacob B.	685 00
Laton, Rachael and Harriet Stanton	841 00
Lawson, Peter	500 00
Lawson Peter	915 00
Lawton, Daniel C	1,000 00
Lay, Darrow	600 00
Lay, Darrow	450 00
Lay, Charles W.	400 00
Lay, Peter, and Smith	450 00

Names of Claimants.	Amount claimed.
Lay, Hiram	$1,500 00
Ledman, John	266 00
Lee, James	750 00
Lee, Gad H., & Philip Donahue	1,800 00
Lee, Gilbert, & Orrin Turner	3,825 00
Leek, Jarvis S.	Not stated
Leek, Jarvis S.	800 00
Leet, Thomas R.	1,710 00
Leicht, Henry	1,385 00
Leid, Barbara (administratrix, &c.)	900 00
Leland, Z. A.	2,310 00
Leland, Z. A.	5,700 00
Lester, Adam	1,051 20
Lester, James	2,025 00
Lewis, Frederick	4,480 00
Lewis, Frederick	400 00
Lewis, Frederick (trustee)	3,200 00
Lewis Hazard, deceased (estate of)	1,800 00
Lewis, Maria	300 00
Lewis, Robert	1,785 00
Lewis, Hiram	1,115 00
Like, Peter H.	640 00
Lincoln, Lucius	620 00
Lincoln, Andrew, et al.	20,500 00
Linder, Frank	300 00
Little, John H.	12,000 00
Little, Savillon	240 00
Locke, James S.	10,488 00
Lockman, Nicholas	256 00
Lockwood, John H.	2,029 00
Loness, Caroline A.	427 20
Loness, Caroline A.	300 00
Loness, Katharine	275 00
Loness, Katharine	108 00
Long, Benjamin H., & H. P. Smith (executors, &c.)	3,271 50
Long, Charles	1,100 00
Long, John	1,000 00

Names of Claimants.	Amount claimed.
Long, John, deceased (heirs of)	$2,450 00
Loomis, William W.	420 00
Lord, William	750 00
Lord, Henry	600 00
Lord, Gilderoy	21,772 00
Lounsbeurry, William	4,900 00
Loveland, Joseph D.	1,181 00
Lovell, Reuben	4,430 00
Lowe, George	883 00
Lucy, Mary Ann	700 00
Lukeman, Christian	725 00
Lureman, John	100 00
Lynch, William	612 00
Lynch, Rosa	100 00
Lyon, Chester J., et al.	750 00
Lyon, Henrietta D.	800 00
Lyon, Lyman R.	7,300 00
Mabee, Simon	1,400 00
Madison, John H.	550 00
Mahar, Lawrence	175 00
Main, James S.	500 00
Mall, John	395 00
Malldame, Mathias	400 00
Mallery, R. C. & Sam. Fappier	3,965 49
Manchester, Mary A.	960 00
Mann, Michael	1,636 00
Manning, William	7,480 00
Marcks, Frederick	80 00
Marley, Richard	1,972 00
Mars, Samuel S.	105 50
Marsh, Charles N.	181 00
Marsh, William	10,000 00
Martin, Rhoda	200 00
Martin, Orry	483 00
Martin, John	125 00
Martin, Philip	1,000 00
Martin, William	800 00

Names of Claimants.	Amount claimed.
Martindale, George C., et al	$200 00
Mathews, Thomas & Son	273 00
Mattison, Nathaniel B	850 00
Mattison, John P	365 00
Mattoon, John P	500 00
Maurris, William T. & Co	832 00
Mayer, Martin	200 00
Mayer, Michael	1,127 00
Mayo, Peter	440 00
McAffrey, Patrick	242 10
McAffrey, Phelix	690 50
McCann, John	3,000 00
McCann, Philip	1,800 00
McCauliff, John (estate of)	659 10
McClintock, Charles	700 00
McColliff, John	400 00
McCollum, Mary E	5,928 38
McCoon, Dennis D	7,150 00
McCormick, Mrs. Anna	250 00
McDonald, James	1,621 25
McDonald, James	960 00
McDougall, John A	2,540 75
McGram, Miles	1,000 00
McGrath, John	1,000 00
McGlone, Patrick	300 00
McGuire, Thomas	1,700 00
McHugh, Patrick	6,000 00
McIntyre, Patrick	355 00
McKee, James	205 00
McKee, Johnson, Mrs	350 00
McKinley, Richard & Co	3,500 00
McKinley, Jesse	8,000 00
McKinney, Patrick	100 00
McKinney, Patrick	100 00
McKinney, John	1,150 00
McLeese, Mary	670 00
McMahon, William	2,000 00

Names of Claimants.	Amount claimed.
McVicar, George W.	$1,000 00
Mead, Jerry	250 00
Meeher, Lewis	315 75
Meeker, Elliott	1,012 00
Meeker, Lewis	175 00
Meesick, John	1,125 00
Melcher, Frederick.	463 00
Merrell and Coleman	220 00
Merrell, Abijah M.	510 00
Merrell, Samuel W.	30 00
Merriam, Ela	54 00
Merrigan, Thomas	134 00
Merry & Breed,	2,500 00
Merry & Breed	26,810 00
Mersereau, J. L.	1,900 00
Mersereau, John F. and G.	5,115 00
Mersereau, George J.	2,390 00
Metrote, Francis	1,175 00
Middleton, Andrew	110 00
Miles, S.	6,781 25
Miles, Sweeting	2,181 25
Miller, Charles	1,150 00
Miller, Addison C.	4,153 10
Miller, Brainard	290 00
Miller, Christian	1,748 00
Miller, Christian F.	490 00
Miller, Ezra	485 60
Miller, George H.	297 50
Miller, Nelson	88 50
Miller, Nelson	633 00
Miller, Nelson	209 75
Miller, Jeremiah T.	100 00
Miller, Sidney B.	310 00
Miller, John	1,000 00
Miller, John	470 00
Miller, Rudolph	177 00
Millington, Thomas & William G. Wilson	1,898 00

Names of Claimants.	Amount claimed.
Millis, Mary Ann	$3,350 00
Millis, Mary Ann	2,300 00
Mills, Lewis H	845 00
Millrite, Christian	376 25
Miltreer, Michael	245 00
Minton, Andrew	75 00
Minton, Andrew	420 00
Minton, Michael (estate of)	1,205 00
Minier, Samuel	4,602 75
Minier, John	6,325 50
Mirrick, A. J	3,300 00
Miser, Joseph, Jr	9,467 93
Mogg, Aaron	3,000 00
Monroe, D. C. & J.	415 00
Monroe, James	438 20
Moll, Augustus	310 00
Moll, Ferdinand	360 00
Montgomery, H. H	4,000 00
Moore, Silas	4,709 00
Moore, John	9,600 00
Moore, George P	9,402 00
Moore, Joseph C	875 00
Moore, Charles	540 00
Moore, John	150 00
Moreland, Parley	138 00
Morgan, Margaret	150 00
Morgan, Louisa	100 00
Morgan, Samuel	6,060 00
Morgan, Conley M	11,115 00
Morgan, Carter H	8,880 00
Morgan, Conley M. & Carter H	500 00
Morrell, Francis	225 00
Morrell, Asa	122 00
Morris, John W	3,000 00
Morris, John W	1,400 00
Morris, Owen H	1,385 50
Morris, Owen H	3,000 00
Morris, Hannah M. & Harriet	100 00

Names of Claimants.	Amount claimed.
Morrison, Nancy	$2,304 00
Morrow, James H. & Co	5,676 56
Morse, Amos	2,200 00
Morse, Charles	300 00
Morse, Harlow	450 00
Morse, Susan	1,560 00
Morton, John and William	600 00
Morton, Thomas	2,800 00
Morton, Thomas	5,803 00
Mossop, Isaac T	250 00
Muck, Jacob	3,751 00
Mulchy, Michael	747 00
Mundy, Nicholas S	3,265 00
Munsell, James	1,922 50
Munson, Samuel A	2,300 00
Murdick, Austin	1,740 00
Murray, Daniel	925 00
Murray, Thomas	1,800 00
Murray, John T	3,000 00
Murray, Mrs. Maria E	168 60
Myers, Francis B	1,862 50
Myers, Jacob	700 00
Myers, John	500 00
Names, John R	1,000 00
National Bank of Auburn	27,500 00
Needham, Benjamin	1,600 00
Neff, Benjamin H	203 00
Neillan, William	400 00
Neville, Alexander	7,540 40
Newbecker, Jacob	618 50
Newbecker, Jacob, Jr	263 50
Newcomb, Moses W	750 00
Newell and Sperry	4,310 00
Newman, Henry	2,000 00
Newman, Henry	2,000 00
Newman, George	217 50
New York and Rome Transportation Company	5,971 37

Names of Claimants.	Amount claimed.
Nichol, William	$1,780 00
Nichols, George	9,668 00
Nichols, John S.	19,146 00
Nichols, John H.	280 00
Nichols, Alexander H.	1,200 00
Nichols, Charles	2,722 50
Nichols, Justus	3,280 00
Nichols, Robert, Jr.	175 00
Niles, James L.	3,781 98
Ninde, Sophronia F.	350 00
Nobinger, Dorothy	1,232 50
Noble, Frederick	1,100 00
Nomander, Isaac S.	255 00
Northrup, Joseph A.	5,800 00
Northrup, George	4,310 77
Norton, Winthrop	535 00
Norton, Winthrop	560 00
Norton, Catharine, (executrix, &c.)	1,140 00
Nutting, Joseph	75 00
Oatman, Reuben C.	345 00
O'Brien, James	4,553 00
O'Brien, James	1,061 00
O'Brien, James	1,000 00
O'Brien, James	2,775 00
O'Brien, Timothy	440 00
O'Brien, Patrick	800 00
O'Connor, Thomas	3,300 00
O'Dougherty, Anna M.	5,433 00
O'Dougherty, Patrick	13,765 75
O'Keeffee, Daniel	262 55
O'Keeffee, Timothy	448 70
Olmstead, Elizabeth	1,322 00
Olmstead & Fish	650 00
Olmstead, Augustus	3,400 00
Olmstead, James F.	1,253 00
Olmstead, Julia M.	2,398 00
Olmstead, Avery	978 00

Names of Claimants.	Amount claimed.
Orman, Orris C	$250 00
Osborn, Hobart	2,500 00
Osborn, W. Otis	1,110 00
Osborn, W. Otis	412 90
Ostrander, Alexander and George Douglas	922 50
Ostrander, Alexander and George Douglas	700 00
Ostrander, Mary Jane T.	1,000 00
Ostrander, Charles A	22 50
Otto, August	45 00
Owens, Ira M	400 00
Owens, Edward	64 50
Paddock, John	7,050 00
Paddock, S. D., Jr	1,200 00
Page, Caroline L	400 00
Page, Caroline Lewis	22,865 00
Page, Caroline L., et al.	3,500 00
Paine, Mary Ann	391 00
Paine, Thomas J	150 00
Paine, William	3,965 00
Palmer, Rufus C	1,000 00
Palms, Amon R	490 00
Pangburn, Charles	1,500 00
Papke, Charles	419 37
Pardee, Myron	47,000 00
Pardee, Myron	12,000 00
Park, Smith	2,245 00
Park, John	2,526 00
Park, George W., et al	414 01
Parker, Hiram	1,800 00
Parker, John	450 00
Parker, Abijah & Susan A. Rogers	650 00
Parish, Eliza J. & John Patten	240 00
Parsons, James A	760 00
Parsons, Stephen M	1,200 00
Partridge, Edward	2,000 00
Patrick, Henry	3,150 00
Patrick, John	100 00

Names of Claimants.	Amount claimed.
Patten, Silas	Not stated
Patten, Silas	$3,750 00
Patterson, William	2,462 00
Patterson, George W.	300 00
Payne, Garrett W.	272 00
Pearse, James	20 00
Pearsall, William S.	3,031 00
Pease, Mary, and Ezra	750 00
Peavy, Betsey	300 00
Peck Ira	2,280 00
Peck, Ira	1,000 00
Peck, Ira	12,485 00
Peck, Ira	1,425 00
Peck, Robert, Jr.	770 00
Pelton, Elizabeth, and son	373 00
Pelton, J. N.	345 50
Pepper, Aaron	950 00
Perinton, Town of	2,000 00
Perkins, Allen	7,100 00
Perrinton, David	2,800 00
Perrine, William D.	5,280 00
Perry, John F.	2,000 00
Pettie, Adaline	175 00
Peters, John	326 00
Petrie, Walter W.	300 00
Pettit, Louisa	31,816 00
Phelps, Ezekial B.	10,529 00
Phillips, Elijah	1,700 00
Phillips, John	452 58
Phillips, Peter	400 00
Pickard, Lucy, et al.	2,600 00
Pickard, A. H.	842 50
Pickard, Henry	1,099 50
Pickard, Lucy	2,275 00
Pickard, Lucy	770 00
Pickard, Philip W.	370 25
Pickard, Albert	345 00

Names of Claimants.	Amount claimed.
Pickard, William	$933 00
Pierce, Albert	1,500 00
Pierce, Elet	1,350 00
Pils, John	185 00
Piron, Jacob	720 00
Pitcher, Edwin	500 00
Plair, Henry	498 00
Platner, Maria	1,000 00
Platt, Thomas C.	6,141 50
Plumb, Ovid	3,496 00
Poor, Matthew (commissioners of highways)	3,250 00
Poor, Andrew	185 00
Portable, Steam Engine and Manufacturing Co.	1,685 00
Porter, Francis	2,400 00
Porter, John	2,700 00
Porter, Monroe P., & Weston	2,500 00
Post, Philo	302 00
Post, Lorenzo S.	900 00
Post, Alanson	2,000 00
Potter, Joseph	5,695 47
Potvin, Joseph	650 00
Potvin, Joseph	476 00
Pouty, Minerva	4,000 00
Powers, John M.	1,330 00
Pratt, L. S. and son	1,188 73
Pratt, Leander S.	3,444 00
Prentice, William	4,634 00
Presley, Harvey N.	57 00
Preslow, James, & Ambrose Kelsey	247 00
Preston, Katharine	700 00
Preston, Thomas, and wife	1,300 00
Probasco, Samuel	2,930 00
Pruyn, J. V. L.	10,700 00
Pryne, Francis	200 00
Pulford, Samuel	3,000 00
Pumpelly, Frederick W. (estate of)	5,078 00
Putman J. L.	3,000 00

Names of Claimants.	Amount claimed.
Putman, Garrett V.	$1,650 00
Purcell, Patrick	400 00
Quillinan, James	1,900 00
Race, Buel	400 00
Raenbolt, Olese	1,270 00
Ragan, John T.	200 00
Ragan, John F.	95 00
Ramsay, Thomas	1,200 00
Ramsdell, Gideon R.	Not stated
Randall, Samuel A.	2,762 00
Ransom, J. F. & Charles Berry	578 00
Rant, Patrick	2,000 00
Ray, Robert (trustee, &c.)	700 00
Ray, Bannister & Co.	3,622 00
Ray, Bannister & Co.	3,622 00
Redell, Charles	130 00
Reed, Richard	1,180 00
Reed, Edmund M.	1,560 00
Reed, E. M.	325 00
Reed, Henry L.	300 00
Reese, Frederick	1,514 00
Regal, Carl	482 70
Remnington Paper Co.	7,980 00
Rensselaer & Saratoga Railroad Co	1,377 75
Rensselaer & Saratoga Railroad Co	3,705 00
Renshaw, Mary	194 00
Renshaw, Samuel B.	278 00
Resha, Peter	125 12
Reynolds, Luther J.	680 00
Reynolds, Nathan	1,000 00
Reynolds, Valentine	1,515 00
Rhines, Christopher B.	363 50
Rhodes, Dexter	750 00
Rhodes, Mary J. (administratrix)	7,360 00
Rice, Augustus	7,645 80
Rice, Luther	300 00
Rice Edwin	4,376 23

Names of Claimants.	Amount claimed.
Rice, David	$2,800 00
Rich, Asa D	60 40
Rich, Frederick	400 00
Richardson, Joel	122 00
Richardson, Wallace	5,650 00
Riley, Thomas	150 00
Rink, William	775 00
Riordan, Baldwin	38 00
Rive, Levi	5,281 80
Robb, James M., deceased (estate of)	1,125 00
Robbins, Dexter E.	4,237 50
Roberts, Maria	775 00
Roberts, Maria (executrix, &c.)	1,500 00
Roberts, John (executors of)	1,300 00
Roberts, Silas G.	4,000 00
Robertson, Samuel	40 00
Robinson, William C.	324 35
Robinson, Elizabeth	653 00
Robinson, Elizabeth H., et al.	583 00
Robinson, R. and son	11,300 00
Robinson, R. and son	6,600 00
Robinson, Robert and son	2,968 40
Robinson, Robert	35,500 00
Rochester & Pittsford Plank Road Co.	557 03
Rochester, City of	19,964 43
Rock Bottom Bridge Co.	560 00
Rodman, Charles	2,425 00
Roe, Jackson T.	3,500 00
Rogers, Patrick	10,359 00
Rogers, Susan, and Abijah Parker	650 00
Roggo, Christian	735 00
Roggo, John, and Gottfried Harpty	600 00
Rome, Watertown & Ogdensburgh Railroad Co.	2,650 00
Root, Artemus	4,739 63
Rose, Orrin W.	1,750 00
Ross, William	800 00
Rose, George E. and Thomas J.	6,060 00

Names of Claimants.	Amount claimed.
Rose, Z.	$2,500 00
Rose, E. P. and Z.	5,000 00
Row, James, Field & Co.	147 00
Rowland, Henry	800 00
Rudd, Prosper E.	494 00
Rudd, Prosper E.	550 00
Rudd, Benjamin.	170 00
Rumsey, John A.	4,500 00
Rumsey, John A.	3,300 00
Rumsey, Edwin S. and George	2,921 00
Runyon, C. F.	261 00
Ryan, Michael	7,165 00
Sahr, Charles	238 00
Sahr, Martin	350 00
Sander, Charles P.	5,786 00
Sanders, Eugens S.	5,310 00
Sanders, Jacob G. (estate of)	6,000 00
Sanders & Tooper	1,070 00
Sayre, Willis B., and others.	11,890 00
Saddlemire, Katharine	1,500 00
Saddlemire, Paul	1,000 00
Sahr, Charles	1,600 34
Sand, Peter J.	900 00
Sanders, Jacob G. (estate of)	5,000 00
Sanders, Charles P.	3,000 00
Sanders, Barent B.	1,500 00
Sanders, Eugene L.	2,500 00
Sanders, Garrett.	40 00
Sandford, Philip.	1,500 00
Saunders, Mary	100 00
Schaffer, John J.	825 00
Schad, Charles H.	245 00
Schelles, John.	435 25
Scheu, Solomon	2,300 00
Schemminger, Constantine	197 50
Schwinger, Rosanna.	1,310 00
Schwinger, Christopher.	7,625 00

Names of Claimants.	Amount claimed.
Schmidt, Wilhelm	$440 00
Schneible, Paul	765 75
Scott, Abel M.	62 20
Schoells, John, Jr.	595 00
Scott, Martin B., and others	2,760 00
Schoppmein, Ernest	5,325 00
Schoonmaker, R. W.	122 50
Schuyler, Rensselaer	412 50
Schoonmaker, Peter	500 00
Schwinger, William	525 00
Schroeppel, Richard	3,000 00
Schroeppel, Mary H.	1,200 00
Schroeppel, Richard	1,175 00
Schroeppel & Bollver	4,000 00
Scott, Martin B., and others	1,500 00
Scott, Daniel H.	110 00
Scott, George H.	125 00
Scott & Nesbitt	9,000 00
Seager, Lewis,	122 00
Seelye, John H.	1,300 00
Seaman, Horace	2,816 20
Seymour, Henry I.	6,810 00
Seamour & Phillips	1,489 00
Seaman & Babcock	1,500 00
Searl, Eliza B.	410 00
Sears, O. M.	795 00
Seekle, Loren	500 00
Seldon, Henry A.	3,069 00
Settle & Jones	162 13
Seymour, Charles	4,772 50
Seymour & Talcott, and William D. Phillips	1,489 00
Seymour, Henry I.	6,848 40
Shattuck, Charles L.	5,000 00
Shalager, John	1,440 00
Shaughnessey, Lawrence	1,282 00
Sherman, George W.	569 00
Shea, Peter	1,060 00

Names of Claimants.	Amount claimed.
Sheehan, Margaret	$1,250 00
Shell, Giles	189 00
Shuts, John	820 00
Sheel Gottfried	1,005 00
Shell, Giles	605 00
Shea, Thomas	78 00
Sheldon, Adelbert S.	48 00
Sheldon, Gardner	742 70
Shine, Patrick	225 00
Shonomen, Adam	745 00
Shultz, Peter	745 00
Shultz, Charles	285 00
Shyer, George	704 00
Shyer, John	1,083 00
Shearman, Jane	5,590 00
Sharp, Peter G.	374 00
Sharlock, Sarah	25 00
Shead & Graves	5,000 00
Shell, Giles	8,691 16
Shepard, Ely	650 00
Shepard, Joshua	415 00
Shepard, Pratt	250 00
Shepard, Henry M.	300 00
Shepard, Joshua	150 00
Shepard, Elisha, and others	8,640 00
Sherman, Wasson & Co	7,252 02
Sherman, R. T. (agent, &c.)	1,500 00
Sherwood, Noah	2,000 00
Shoemaker, Andrew	1,311 00
Shullr, James D. (estate of)	5,000 00
Simpson, John	821 50
Sibley, Furman S.	444 00
Simmons, Aaron	173 00
Sickwault, Jacob	2,365 00
Silsby, H. C.	7,000 00
Silver, William	114 13
Simmons, Elizabeth	652 00

Names of Claimants.	Amount claimed.
Simpson, John	$2,125 00
Sinclair, F. A.	108 00
Sinclair, F. A.	873 75
Skinner, Charles P.	1,150 00
Skaneateles Iron Works	7,820 00
Skinner, Horace, and W. Y.	887 85
Skut, Hiram	375 00
Sleeper, Thomas C. (agent)	9,016 00
Sloat, Alby	1,060 00
Slade, Benjamin J	1,500 00
Slocum, Arnold	874 00
Slocum, Arnold	6,590 00
Smith, Benjamin W.	620 00
Smith, Charles	3,272 50
Smith, Horace W	5,500 00
Smith, Russell (estate of)	1,827 00
Smith, Marietta	250 60
Smith & Wildrick	169 00
Smith, Lua	1,500 00
Smith, Abigail	875 00
Smith, Alonzo G.	1,455 00
Smith, Horace C	575 00
Smith, William	133 50
Smith, Anna	301 00
Smith Charles	675 00
Smith, Mary	460 00
Smith & Spaulding	1,300 00
Smith, Charles C.	1,330 00
Smith, Ezekiel	263 00
Smith, Ezekiel	747 00
Smalley, Jerome M.	68 00
Smith, Willis P.	220 00
Smith, Delvis	1,050 75
Smith, Benjamin P	120 00
Smith, & Blaisdell	6,000 00
Smith, William	2,000 00
Smith, James D	150 00

Names of Claimants.	Amount claimed.
Smith, Labon J	$6,015 00
Smith, Ryal Y	7,055 00
Smith, George, and heirs of W. Smith, deceased	8,750 00
Smith, Wanton	133 00
Snell, Christian	1,200 00
Snell, John	1,161 50
Snyder, Henry, D. H., Jr	49,701 02
Snyder, Joseph M	1,712 00
Southard, Lester	1,000 00
Spencer, Margaret	508 00
Spencer, Ezekiel	3,350 00
Spencer, James D	2,500 00
Sperry, R. S. (assignee, &c.)	3,000 00
Spies George	207 00
Springsted, Jacob	350 00
Squire, Charles D	429 50
Starbuck, James F	6,000 00
Standring, John T	298 00
Stanton, Egbert	825 00
Standering, Leonard S	142 50
Staples, S. G	330 00
Starr, Henry M., and Irwin M	4,000 00
States, Patrick	437 00
Stevenson, J. M	500 00
Stewart, David A	1,350 00
Stewart, Norman J	400 00
Stella, Aaron	6,250 00
Stiles, Alfred	1,015 25
Stiles, Alfred	8,700 00
Stiles, Jared	71 38
Stiles, Jared	2,350 00
Stiles, Jared, Alfred and Dwight	9,100 00
Stone, James M	125 00
Stone, Ira A	25 00
Sturm, Peter J	150 00
Storrs, Francis A	10,510 00
Stanberger, George	520 00

Names of Claimants.	Amount claimed.
Stanton, Samuel H	$350 00
Stark, Elverton C	600 00
Stark, Michael	15 96
Stanber, Henry	65 00
Stein, Robert	985 00
Stein, Thomas	1,773 00
Stephen, Frederick	205 00
Stearns, Josiah A	3,192 40
Sterling, John A	908 96
Storm Uri	1,280 00
Stevens, William P	892 50
Stebbins, Frank G	104 00
Storrs, Alexander	290 00
Stoven, Michael	3,230 00
Stock, John	285 00
Strong, E. Benedict	600 00
Stack, James	350 00
Starks, Betsey	350 00
Stillwater, Town of	750 00
Story, Hugh	440 00
Story, Hugh	987 50
Steele, Aaron	2,982 50
Steele & Jennings	8,338 00
Strich, John	910 00
Sumner, Hiram B	175 00
Sullivan & Glancey	330 00
Sullivan, Timothy	220 00
Susquehanna Bridge Company	1,000 00
Sumner, Alanson A	2,500 00
Sumner, Alanson A	1,000 00
Supervisor of Little Falls et al	15,000 00
Susan, Henry	1,310 00
Swinnerton, John M	450 00
Swan, Robert J	1,500 00
Sweeney, James and others	2,000 00
Sweet, George	1,920 00
Swobe, Jacob	1,650 00

Names of Claimants.	Amount claimed.
Syracuse Peat and Marl Company	$18,000 00
Syron, M. Barton	500 00
Syron, Abram B	500 00
Syron, M. Coleman	500 00
Talcott & Seymour (executors) and Richard Evans	1,535 00
Tangley, John	345 30
Taylor, Emily G	9,965 00
Teller, Benjamin F	1,360 00
Terpenny, George	1,500 00
Terry, John G	800 00
Thayer, J. & Co	295 35
Thiebolt, Barbara	1,400 00
Thorman, John	323 00
Thuresson, Andrew	4,402 50
Thomas, John J	353 75
Thomas, John J	660 00
Thomas, Didymus	2,777 00
Thompson, Sophia R	285 00
Thurber, Frederick C	1,410 00
Tilley, John	20,000 00
Tibbits, Elizabeth	2,500 00
Tilley, John	6,000 00
Timmerman, Frederick	640 00
Tinney, Carlton K	7,800 00
Titcomb, Stephen	1,000 00
Titus, D. S	800 00
Torrey, French	9,000 00
Torrey, Royal U	15,000 00
Torrey, Royal U	200 00
Torrey, Royal U	10,000 00
Towns of Hounsfield and Brownville	2,600 00
Towns of Greig and Leyden	2,107 00
Townsend, Harvey	2,430 00
Townsend, Justus and James H	6,000 00
Townsend, Ingrahm	9,020 00
Townsend, Ingrahm	9,020 00
Townsend, Ingrahm	365 00

Names of Claimants.	Amount claimed.
Towers, Julius C	$480 00
Toohey, William	802 00
Tool, James	555 00
Tobin, James	1,000 00
Town of Cuba	1,040 70
Town of Hinsdale	1,073 35
Tousley, William	1,329 40
Tracey, Benjamin F	101 50
Traffarn, Job and L	5,419 00
Traffarn, J. L. & Co	2,626 00
Traver, Martin	900 00
Travis, James	920 00
Tripp, John	1,675 00
Travers, John	200 00
Tremain, Cyrus F	290 00
Trimball, John	500 00
Truman & Banks	3,136 74
Turrell, Mary C	1,430 00
Tully, Patrick	1,763 00
Tuttle, Salmon	2,270 00
Turrel, Peter P	735 00
Tuller, Mahala L	1,000 00
Tyler, William A	1,300 00
Tyler, Charlotte	170 00
Tyler, Orrin	500 00
Ultsh, Andrew	801 40
Ulrick, Martin	1,050 00
Underhill, Bloomer	375 00
Underhill, Bloomer	68 00
Underhill, G. A	105 00
Underhill, George A	237 50
Upham, Joseph	593 87
Urban, George	743 00
Utica Cotton Co	18,639 00
Van Schoyck, Elias	1,940 00
Van Slyck, Alvin	970 00
Van Slyke, Alvin	665 00

Names of Claimants.	Amount claimed.
Van Evera, John R.	$2,000 00
Van De Bogart, Nicholas and Giles Y.	2,029 00
Vandervoort, Jackson D.	475 00
Vanderburgh, Nicholas.	4,562 00
Van Schaick, Mary Ann.	1,130 00
Vail, Mary B.	469 00
Vallmer, Philip.	1,000 00
Vanamee, Smith.	658 00
Van Arnam, Wm. C.	1,200 00
Van Arnam, Wm. C.	2,250 00
Van Benthuysen, John.	8,020 00
Van Brocklin, Stephen A.	1,000 00
Van Cleef, J. and others, heirs, &c.	1,000 00
Van Cleef, William G.	1,800 00
Van Epps, Robert.	300 00
Van Kirk, Amos.	600 00
Van Kirk, Betsey.	2,000 00
Van Kirk, Mary, (heirs of).	800 00
Van Nevery, William.	1,500 00
Van Valkenburgh, C. and A.	125 00
Van Valkenburgh, John.	352 80
Van Valkenburgh, Elias.	112 00
Van Vranken, Turtuler.	5,000 00
Van Vranken, Turtuler.	2,000 00
Vaughan, John J.	1,525 00
Veber, C. C.	8,983 00
Vedder, John A.	2,000 00
Vincent, Charles.	755 00
Vickers, William H.	120 00
Vignerson, Mary Ann.	1,090 00
Vincent, Herbert B*.	1,080 00
Voorhees, Catharine Ann.	1,196 00
Voorhees, John H.	900 00
Vollmer, Charles.	2,957 00
Vollmer, Daniel.	100 00
Voorhees, James L.	1,814 55
Voorhees, Peter (amended claim).	8,947 91

Names of Claimants.	Amount claimed.
Voorhees, Peter	$1,200 00
Warmwood, John	5,100 00
Walsh, Michael	2,000 00
Wadsworth, James S. (estate of)	2,982 00
Waite, Leander R.	285 00
Waite, Leander R.	2,000 00
Watson, John	3,400 00
Wall, Theodocia	27,300 00
Watertown Paper Co.	1,580 00
Warren, Lafayette	2,533 25
Waldurf, Peter	1,200 00
Walker, Peter	250 00
Walsh, Thomas	420 00
Ward, Alvah, A. McVicker and J. G. Wood (contractors)	13,700 00
Ward, Alvah and A. McVicker	1,205 00
Ward & McVicker	8,625 00
Warmort, Anna E.	195 00
Water commission of city of Watertown	9,700 00
Watertown (city of)	3,300 00
Wendt, William	70 00
Wendt, William	197 50
Weeks, Forrest G.	329 70
Westphal, Carl	652 25
Wernersbeck, Jacob	311 00
Weiland, William	575 00
Wehnung, Philip	1,615 00
Wemple, Cornelius	500 00
Wendle, Jacob	75 00
West, Abiel	1,465 00
West & Taggert	850 00
Weller, Gertrude	2,000 00
Weeks, Hiram	2,730 00
Webster, William	260 00
Welch, John	448 50
Webber, Charles	455 00
Webster, Lewis L.	1,850 00

Names of Claimants.	Amount claimed.
Weed, W. J.	$1,600 00
Weilman, Jacob	150 00
Welch, Minerva Mrs.	675 00
Weich, John, (estate of)	1,200 00
Wemple, Cornelius	500 00
Wendt, William	612 18
Wentworth, Sylvanus	60 00
Wengert, Daniel	400 00
Wentgert, Henry	150 00
West, Abial	100 00
Westbrook, J., & J. Morehouse*	500 00
West, Zelinda & J. A. Page	1,000 00
Weston, Nathaniel	1,000 00
Weller, Leonard	252 00
Wells, Charles	1,050 00
Wetherston, Daniel	500 00
Wethey, Erastus	175 00
Wetmore, Gideon	6,600 00
Wheeler, Solomon	780 85
Wheeler, George W., (estate of)	616 00
White & Wait	1,582 50
White, Daniel	500 00
White, Aaron	2,970 00
White, Jenkins	720 00
Whitney, Virgel	6,100 00
Whitcomb, Judah	3,772 00
Whaling, Thomas	260 00
Wheatley, William	1,500 00
Wheeler, Eunice	157 00
Wheeler, John	1,300 00
White, Edwin C	425 00
White, Truman M	332 00
White, Daniel	400 00
Whitney, Virgil	2,000 00
Whitney, Horace	2,000 00
Whitney, Mary	7,000 00
Williams, Samuel	1,000 00

Names of Claimants.	Amount claimed.
Williams, Orrin P.	$370 00
Williams, Edward	6,700 00
Wiggins, Alexander	115 00
Wilke, Martin	86 00
Wiggins, Robert,	610 00
Wiggins, Robert	800 00
Williams, Stephen	3,293 60
Wing, Orrin	300 00
Williams, George	320 00
Wilcox, M. and H	2,750 00
Wicks, Federick	2,182 50
Wilder, Seth	100 00
Wilder, Seth	6,050 00
Wilke, Martin F	449 88
Wilkes, Michael	658 88
Willis, Benjamin and Riason	4,200 00
Willis, Hannah and Sabia	1,600 00
Willis, Willet R., Jr	1,770 00
Williams, Platt	16,250 00
Williams, Caleb J	452 50
Williams, Luther	500 00
Williamson, Daniel R	500 00
Williams, Esther	500 00
Wilson, Hill H	300 00
Wilson, William	5,885 00
Wilson, William & James Stewart	4,171 62
Wilson, James H	500 00
Wilson, Lyman H	450 00
Wilson, Orville G	400 00
Wilcox, William H	60 00
Winans, Abram	2,250 00
Winans, Aaron (estate of)	1,000 00
Winter, Gabriel L	5,115 00
Wilson, George A	62 00
Wingoo, Allen	150 00
Witherby, Clark	2,606 00
Woolworth, Eugene B. (guardian)	920 00

Names of Claimants.	Amount claimed.
Woodhul, Calvin	$625 50
Wood, A. & Son	3,220 00
Wood, William W. & George Spies	500 00
Wolf, George	2,037 00
Woolf, Jacob, Jr	2,109 00
Wollenberg, Christian	1,065 00
Wollenberg, William	460 00
Wormley, John C	260 00
Woodruff, Julia B	50 00
Wood, Solomon	825 00
Wright, Alice	1,401 60
Wright, George A., Jr	1,080 00
Wright, Alice	282 00
Wright, Lyman and others	2,690 00
Wright, Alice,	780 00
Wright, Charles T	900 00
Wright, Charles T	1,350 00
Wright, Luther	19,680 16
Wurl, William	2,180 25
Wynant, Jacob	100 00
Wyard & Warner	1,525 00
Yaw, George R	1,182 50
Yates, John	3,590 00
Yates, Lorenzo	2,000 00
Yates, Lorenzo	5,000 00
Yerdon, Albert	500 00
Yeomans, Andrew J	158 60
Youmans, Anthony	1,000 00
Young, William A	4,000 00
Zabal, John	210 00
Zabal, John	180 00
Zabal, William	190 00
Zink, Andrew	687 45
Zink, John	805 25

STATEMENT

SHOWING THE AMOUNT ALLOWED BY THE CANAL BOARD IN CASES APPEALED TO THEM FROM THE DECISION OF THE CANAL APPRAISERS.

Name of Claimants.	Amount allowed.
Ackerman, Herman	$1,746 46
Haskins, James P.	13,883 50
Hagar & Toskey	1,493 50
Loomis & Griswold,	187 45
McCann, John	1,910 61
McKinley, Jesse	2,980 00
Mesereau, George J	2,155 40
Palmer, George W	852 00
Peck, Ira	834 80
White, Amos C	852 00
Writers, Gabriel W	2,989 97

ERRATA.

Page 4. Black River Claims. The words "*See Senate Digest of* 1869" were a marginal note, and should not have been inserted.

Page 20. Erskine G. Clark and others. At the end of Legislative Action upon said claim, the following should be added:

A bill for the relief of these claimants was introduced into the Assembly in 1870 and passed both Houses, but was not signed by the Governor, jurisdiction having been conferred upon the Canal Appraisers by general law. (See chapter 321 of Laws of 1870.)

After page 81, the following should be added:

Thomas McLean. Nature of claim: Papers not on file and nature of claim unknown.

Legislative action: Senate Journal, 1870. Petition presented and referred to the committee on claims, 143.

INDEX TO DIGEST OF CLAIMS.

1870.

A.

	PAGE.
Aash, Thomas	1, 9
Adams, Charles H	1
Alden, Walter S	1, 20
Alliger, Thomas C	1
Amsterdam and Port Jackson (trustee of,)	2
Anderson, George B	2
Anderson, John	2
Angel, Rensselaer W	3
Anthon, John H	3
Avery, L. G	3
Awards by Canal Appraiser	143
Awards by Canal Board	143

B.

Babcock, H. H. and Son	3
Bagley and Sewall	4
Bailey, Franklin	4, 9
Bailey, Harden	4, 9
Bangs, Myron	4, 110
Banks, Alonzo	4, 95, 96
Barhydt, Nicholas	4
Barkley, Alexander	5
Barker, Peter	6
Barnes, John	5, 21
Barrett, Z. W	6
Beebe, Eloisa O	6, 109
Billing, Charles	6, 115, 116
Bellows, James	7, 73
Bennett, Albert	7
Berry Charles	7
Berry, Zurah	8, 118
Biddlecome, Olive	8, 15

	PAGE.
Billinghurst, Lucien	8
Bissell, Walter	9, 57
Blaisdell, John C.	9
Blood, John	10
Botsford, Augustus	10, 95, 96
Bradley, George B.	11, 79
Bradley, M. N.	11
Bread, Daniel	11
Breed, George G. and Oliver	11, 135
Briggs, H. S.	12
Bronson, Eli A.	12
Brooks, Enos C.	13
Bruon, Henry	9, 14
Buckley, Timothy	14, 20
Burrows, Roswell S.	14
Burton, David, Phebe and Ola	14, 15
Burton, Joseph J.	15
Butterfield, Oliver	9, 10, 15

C.

Calrow, Richard, Jr.	15
Campbell, James and John	16, 21
Card, Stephen	15, 16
Carlton, Orvill N.	16, 20
Carman, George	16
Carman, Charles	17
Case, Charles E.	17
Case, Lorenzo	18
Case, Samuel F.	18, 63
Caston, Charles C.	23, 95, 96
Catlin, Nicholas M.	18, 20
Chadwick, John	18, 19, 115, 116
Chamberlain, Calvin T.	19
Clark, B. H.	21
Clark, Erskine G. (see errata)	20
Clark, Linus R.	19
Coe, Samuel	22, 95, 96
Cole, William	22, 118
Coleman, James M.	22, 117
Collamer, Charles A.	22
Conley, John W.	23
Cotter, Daniel	24
Craft, Elizabeth	24
Crandall, Charlotte M.	21, 25
Crandal, Enos T.	25
Crane, Ambrose	21, 25

	PAGE.
Crowley, Timothy 20,	25
Crum, Nathan......................	26
Curtis, C. W......................	26
Curtis, Horatio N..................	26
Cuyler, George M..................	27

D.

	PAGE.
Daggett, Mary E...................	27
Daley, Bryan 20,	28
Daly, Terrence 9, 10,	28
Daly, Walter......................	28
Dallamir, Thomas..................	28
Danolds, C. A.....................	28
Danube (town of)..................	29
Davidson, John 20,	29
Davis Sewing Machine Co...........	29
Davis, Charles	29
Dean, William 30, 95,	96
DeForrest, Gerardus................	30
DeGraw, C. J......................	30
DeGraw, Charles J................ 31,	48
Delong, H. V......................	32
Dewey, Asahel P................ 9,	32
Dewey, C..........................	32
Deyer, John G.....................	32
Dibble, Horace 20,	33
Dickerman, Elizabeth...............	33
Dickinson, Elizabeth................	33
Dinsmore, George	33
Donaldson, Charles A...............	34
Donaldson, Samuel	34
Dougherty, P. O...................	35
Dudley, George F............... 9,	35
Dunn, Margrette...................	35
Dunham, J. A. and W. J............	36
Dygert, Andrew....................	36

E.

	PAGE.
Eaton, Lewis H................ 37,	110
Edwards, Edward H................	37
Edward, John.....................	38
Efner, George B...................	39
Eldred, Rufus.....................	39
Evans, Griffith & Co...............	40

F.

	Page.
Failing, George H.	40
Fay, John D.	40
Ferris, Benjamin	20, 40
Fifty-fifth Regiment	41
Finck's Basin Bridge	41
Fisk, John M.	42
Fitzpatrick, John	42, 43
Fitzhugh, D. H.	42
Fitch, Charles T. and Nelson	42, 87
Flint, Elizabeth	21, 44
Flood, Jeremiah	44
Forest Lumber and Stave Company	45
Fort Hunter Suspension Bridge Company	45
Fowler, L. Jane B.	15, 45
Frasier, Charles E.	46
Frink, Charles G.	46
Fritz, William	47, 115, 116
Frost, A.	47
Fullerton, William S.	13, 47
Fultonville and Johnstown Plank Road Company	47

G.

Gage, Charles H. and James H.	48
Gale, Thomas	48, 49
Gallagher, James	49
Gallagher, Thomas	20, 50
Gay, Edward	20, 50
Gillet and Clarke	50
Gills, Lucius	50
Gilson, Thomas	51
Gilson, E. G.	51, 117
Glass, Joseph J.	51, 135
Goodwill, L.	51, 96
Gordon, John	51, 52
Gorskoff, Frederick	52, 115, 116
Goundrill, William	53
Groff, Phillip	53
Graham, John	9, 53
Grattan, Patrick	53
Green, Martin	54, 118
Green, Job, Jr.	54, 92
Greenwood, Thomas	54
Griffin, Shimel	9, 54
Guarin, Daniel	20, 54
Guarin, James	20, 54
Gutches, Ellen A.	17, 55

H.

	PAGE.
Hadcock, Solomon	55
Haight, Sarah	55
Hall, Charles	55
Hall and Maltby	55
Halley, George	9, 56
Hammond, Charles	56
Hanchett, W. C.	56
Hanks, Byron M.	56, 112
Harden, Samuel H.	9, 56
Harris, Joseph H.	20, 56
Harris, T. Franklin	15, 57
Hart, Amasa P.	57, 135
Harvey, John	57
Hawley, L. T.	58
Hawn, John W.	58
Hayden, Charles J.	58
Henry Mary	20, 59
Henry, John G.	20, 59
Henry, William	20, 59
Herford, George	20, 59
Hern, Jeremiah	59
Hess, Solomon	60
Hoar, Charles B.	61
Hoard Spinn Company	60
Hoard, Pitt	61
Hoffman, Gotlieb	61, 95, 96
Holbrook, Amariah	61
Hollister, William	40, 62
Hope, A. S.	62
Hopkins, Edwin P.	61, 135
Hosch, John F.	63
Hotchkin, B. F. and Son	64
Howell, Edwin W.	64, 95, 96
Howland, Augustus	64, 87
Hubbard, David	64, 135
Hudson, Thomas	64
Heustis, Ephraim P.	9, 64
Huggins, William	6, 65
Humphrey, John M.	65
Hunt, John	65, 105
Hurlburt, Lewis B.	65, 100

I.

Ingalls, George S.	9, 10, 66

J.

	Page.
Jacobs, Daniel C.	66, 115, 116
Jackson, Henry G.	66
Johnson, James	20, 67
Johnson, Jefferson	8, 9, 67, 105
Jones, Robert R.	15, 67

K.

Kelley, Isaac	67, 95, 96
Kimball, V. T.	67
Kincaid, Alexander	9, 10, 68
Kingsbury, John	68, 95, 96
Kissam, A. and Son	69
Knapp, Erastus	8, 9, 69, 105
Knowlton and Brother	69
Krall, William	70, 115, 116

L.

Lamb, Robert	70
Larkin, E. D.	70, 117
Lawson, Peter	20, 70
Ledyard, Jonathan D.	70, 120
Leet, Thomas R.	70
Limestone Creek	71
Lincoln, Andrew W., Charter W. and Josiah K.	71
Little Falls (town of)	72
Liverpool Coarse Salt Company	49, 72
Lock, James S.	72, 95, 96
Loomis, A.	72
Lord, Jarvis	73
Lord, G.	74
Loss, Lewis M.	74
Lovett, Aaron	75
Lyon, W. R. and W. W.	15, 75

M.

Machan, Thomas	75
Manheim (town of)	41, 75
Manning, William	76
Marsh, Walter W.	76, 100
Martin, Russell	76, 77
Matteson, John P.	20, 78
Maxwell, Julia M.	78, 109
McArnary, Mary Ann	78
McArthur, Archibald	78
McBurney, John	79
McClary, Wm.	79

	PAGE.
McGeary, Daniel... 80,	100
McHenry, Francis E... 80,	109
McIntyre, Patrick... 20,	80
McKee, Alexander... 20,	80
McKeever, Mary..	81
McLean, Thomas. (See errata.)	
Mead and Graves..	81
Meeker, Elliott.. 81, 95,	96
Melcher, Frederick...................................... 81, 115,	116
Merry, Edmund.. 81,	135
Militia Officers...	81
Miller, A. C...	82
Miller, Christian.. 82, 115,	116
Miller, John C... 9,	82
Miller, Nelson... 20,	82
Miller, Sidney B. and Jeremiah H........................... 20,	83
Millis, Mary Ann..	83
Mills, M. H... 28,	83
Minton, Michael... 9,	83
Moak, T. W..	84
Moore, Joseph C.. 9,	84
Moore, S...	84
Morduff, Mortimer C... 21,	84
Morgan and Ames..	84
Mott, Samuel L..	84
Moulter, Herrick and Company................................	85
Mudgett, William... 66, 74,	85
Muir, Joseph...	85
Mulchy, Michael..	85
Munro, David A.. 86,	118
Munro, John C... 86,	118
Murray, Edward.. 53,	86
Murray, Hamilton.. 87,	120
Murray, M. E...	86
Murray, Thomas..	87
Mynders, Edward...	87

N.

Nichols, John S...	88
Nichols, Robert, Jr... 9,	87
Nightingale, William... 88,	117
Ninde, Sophronia F...	88
Nine Mile Creek (owners of property on)....................	89

O.

Oatman, Reuben C... 20,	89
Ogden, David...	90

P.

	Page.
Papke, Charles	90, 115, 116
Park, E. W.	90
Parker, Andrew	20, 90
Parsons, Cornelius R.	21, 91
Pattan, James	91, 117
Peck, Robert J.	20, 91
Petrie, William & Co.	91
Pettitt, Louisa R.	92
Pickard, Albert H.	92
Pickard, Lucy, L. A. and P. H	93
Piron, Jacob	93
Phelps, George W.	94
Platt, J. C.	94, 117
Plumb, Ovid	95
Pool, Laura A.	96
Port Leyden Iron Company	97
Portable Steam Engine Company	97
Porter, S. D.	21, 97
Potvin, Joseph	20, 97
Pratt, L. S.	98
Preston, James	98, 118
Pulver, Anthony	98

Q.

Quinn, George	98

R.

Ransom, John F.	99
Raymond, Hezekiah L.	99
Reed, Burton J.	99
Reed, Richard	100
Reed, William W.	100
Regel, Charles	101, 115, 116
Remington Paper Company	101
Reynolds, James G.	101
Reynolds, Nathan	102
Rhodes, Mary J.	95, 96, 102
Richards, Thomas P.	68, 102
Richmond Abram and Seth M.	103
Riley, John	53, 103
Roberts, John	103
Roberts, John S.	104
Roberts, Silas G.	103
Robertson, Mary	104
Rochester City	104
Rose, George	105, 106

	PAGE.
Rose, Orrin W.	8, 9, 105
Rowe, S. B.	105, 118
Rumsey, George and Edwin S.	95, 96, 106

S.

Sage, Albert G.	31, 106
Sahr, Charles	107, 115, 116
Sauer, George W.	107
Saunders, George P.	108
Sayles, Oney	108
Sayre, James W.	108, 109
Sayre, Matthew	109
Sayre, Willis B.	109
Shafer, John	110
Schuyler, Aaron	110
Scovill, Joseph A.	110
Seamen, Horace	95, 96, 111
Second Regiment National Guard	111
Selye, Lewis	112
Seneca Indians	113
Seymour, Elmira	114, 117
Seymour, Henry I.	113
Seymour, McNeil	115, 132
Sharp, Daniel	98, 115
Shea, Peter	100, 115
Shearman, Jane	115, 130
Shell, Giles	115
Sheridan, John	21, 117
Sherrill, George B.	61, 117
Sherrill, James H.	117
Sherwood, E. D.	117
Shuler, James D.	118
Sinclair, John	95, 96, 118
Skaneateles Outlet	119
Sleeper, Thomas C.	95, 96, 119
Smith, Ezekiel	20, 119
Smith, Edmund H.	121
Smith, Gerritt	120
Smith, Laura P.	120
Smith, Mary A., Maria, Joseph and Susan M.	15, 121
Snook, Clark	121
Snyder, H. D. H., Jr.	123
Spencer, Ezekiel	122
Spalding, Lyman A.	123
Sparks, Isaac	123
Spies, George	124

	PAGE.
Stack, James	20, 124
Starbuck, James F.	124
Stearns, Josiah A.	95, 96, 124
Sterling, John A.	95, 96, 124
Storms, Henry	122
Story, Hugh	20, 124
Strong, E. Benedict	100, 125
Supplement containing awards	143
Swan, Lorenzo E.	125
Swartwout, Bernardus	42, 43, 125
Swinerton, John M.	100, 125

T.

Ten Broeck, Henry H.	126
Ten Broeck, Maria	126
Thompson, Elijah	117, 128
Thompson, Elizabeth	127
Thompson, William T.	21, 127
Thorn, William	128
Thurber, Benjamin F.	128
Tilley, John	129
Toole, James	20, 129
Traffam, Job and Leander	129
Treman & Banks	95, 96, 129
Tuttle, Charles M.	87, 130

U.

Underhill, George A. and Bloomer	20, 130
Utica Cotton Company	130

V.

Van De Bogart, Giles and Nicholas	131
Van Namee & Smith	131
Vernam, Amelia C.	132
Veeder, E. E.	118, 132
Vischer, John	133
Volmer, Charles	133
Vulcan Iron Works	133

W.

Wadsworth, Craig B.	43, 134
Wagner, Andrew and Daniel	96, 134
Wait, Eben B.	134
Wall, Theodocia	135
Warren, J. B.	15, 136
Watertown Lock Works	136

	PAGE.
Watertown Paper Company	136
Weatherby, Charles	136
Weeks, Hiram	136
Weiss, Charles	137
Wendt, William	115, 116, 137
West & Taggert	138
Westlake, John E	138
Whitcomb, Judah	95, 96, 138
Whiting, Myron	117, 138
Whitney, Lucy E	15, 139
Wiggins, Robert	20, 139
Wilcox, Mary H	21, 139
Wilke, Martin	115, 116, 139
Willard, Samuel D	139
Williams, Charles P	140
Williams, Stephen	95, 96, 140
Wilson, William	140
Wood, Samuel	20, 140
Woodruff, M. C	141
Wormley, John G	8, 9, 141
Wright, William	115, 116, 141
Wright, Charles T	9, 141
Wurl, William L	115, 116, 141

Y.

Yates, Lorenzo	142
Yaw, George R	149

www.ingramcontent.com/pod-product-compliance
Lightning Source LLC
Chambersburg PA
CBHW070734160426
43192CB00009B/1430